Secrets of

SECRETS
OF
SHADOW LANE

a novella

C. K. Harris

C. K. Harris © 2024
All rights reserved
ISBN: 9781963100303

This is a work of fiction. Names, characters, businesses, events, and incidents are the products of the author's imagination. Any resemblance to actual persons, living or dead, or actual events is purely coincidental.

Secrets of Shadow Lane

*Thank you to Kay C. and Brian Arnold
for your support during the writing of this book.*

What they're saying:

"Secrets of Shadow Lane" by C.K. Harris is an intriguing novel that will captivate readers until the very end. The story follows Sofia, a writer for the Chocotouring magazine, who returns to her home in the picturesque community of Shadow Lane in Dallas after a breakup with her short-term love, Nick.

The book opens with a vivid description of the beauty of Shadow Lane, setting the scene for Sofia's anticipated return to a peaceful routine. However, she quickly realizes that things have changed. Her new neighbors prove to be a source of constant trouble. Among them are Jet and Destiny, a mysterious couple, and a middle-aged woman named Taylor. Jet, in particular, seems dangerous and unnerving, often confronting Sofia in a manner that is unsettling yet seemingly friendly.

Taylor, on the other hand, is convinced that Jet is behind her troubles. She frequently accuses him of trespassing on her property at night and engaging in bizarre activities inside her house. The mystery surrounding Jet and Taylor's accusations against him keeps Sofia on edge and the readers guessing.

The author skillfully weaves an engaging plot that holds the reader's attention from start to finish. The characters are well-developed and unique, each contributing significantly to the story's essence. Sofia is portrayed as a strong, independent woman who faces challenges head-on with minimal support. Her character adds depth to the narrative, making her journey compelling and relatable.

The book is also infused with humor, which adds a delightful layer to the plot. Jet's pranks, though sometimes annoying, are often hilarious, providing comic relief in the midst of tension. The interactions between Taylor, Analise, and Sofia are particularly intriguing and add to the story's dynamic. "Secrets of Shadow Lane" is meticulously edited, with no noticeable errors, enhancing the reading experience. Overall, I thoroughly enjoyed this book and found nothing to dislike. It is a well-crafted story that I would rate 5 out of 5 stars.

Gladis Ratish-Kumar, Online Book Club

Harris skillfully crafts a compelling story, with well-developed characters that contribute greatly to the story's depth. Sofia emerges as a strong and independent heroine, whose journey is connected and interesting. The humor that flows through the novel, especially through Jet's performances, adds some fun to the whole story, temporarily easing the suspense.

Also, "Secrets of Shadow Lane" is flawlessly edited, enhancing the reading experience for the audience. Overall, the book is a well-crafted story that earns a solid 5 out of 5 stars. A master storyteller, Harris ensures that readers are kept thoroughly entertained from beginning to end.

Muqadas Mahnoor, Online Book Club

Reviewed by Pikasho Deka for Readers' Favorite

Secrets of Shadow Lane is an urban drama by C.K. Harris. After spending some time with her boyfriend Nick in Los Angeles, Sofia Lanera realizes their relationship is incompatible and returns home to Shadow Lane in Dallas. However, she quickly discovers that her neighbors in the next-door duplex are no longer the same. She meets Jet, an ex-convict recently released from prison, and his girlfriend, Destiny, an exotic dancer at a club, and doesn't get a good impression of either of them. Meanwhile, her neighbor in Duplex B, Taylor, is becoming increasingly paranoid due to the mind games and pranks played on him by Jet. But Taylor also has a history, and now an FBI agent is in the mix. Will Sofia find the peace she's been looking for in her home ever again?

Secrets of Shadow Lane is a riveting slice-of-life story with mystery and intrigue. There is a palpable sense of suspense and tension that C.K. Harris brings to the narrative that keeps your eyes glued to the pages. As a reader, you're never quite sure what's going to happen next but know it will be fascinating. The author also infuses some psychological thriller elements that make the story unpredictable. Sofia is a likable protagonist who readers will find easy to relate to. Her willingness to help Taylor clashes with her frustration at Taylor's unhinged paranoia, and it adds some complex layers to her character. I was also pleasantly surprised by the amount of humor sprinkled throughout the book, often in small doses of dark comedy. All in all, a very entertaining novel for readers of mystery and drama.

Table of Contents

Chapter 1 - The Neighborhood and The Eviction 1

Chapter 2 – The New Neighbors 9

Chapter 3 – The Ruby Chocolate Story 15

Chapter 4 – The Irish Pub and The Ex-Convict 19

Chapter 5 – The Neighbor Taylor and Her Computer 25

Chapter 6 – The Fence and Cicadas 30

Chapter 7 – The Garage Door and Taylor's Security 33

Chapter 8 – The Robbery and The Oily Wall 38

Chapter 9 – The Poolside Party and Halloween 44

Chapter 10 – The FBI Surveillance 51

Chapter 11 – The DPD Officer and The Pesticide 55

Chapter 12 – The Kidnapping 60

Chapter 13 – The Women's Clothes and The Gun Show 66

Chapter 14 – The Honky Tonk and The Flowerpots 73

Chapter 15 – The Chocolate Tour and The Mushrooms 79

Chapter 16 – The Nudist Neighbor and The Alley Crash 85

Chapter 17 – The FBI and Agent Lawson 89

Chapter 18 – The Taylor Meltdown and Ghost in the Attic 93

Chapter 19 – The Taylor Interview and Treatment 99

Chapter 20 – The Dinner with Lawson 102

Chapter 21 – The Third Date 108

Chapter 1 - The Neighborhood and The Eviction

When evening falls, Shadow Lane gives the impression of a Van Gogh painting, serene on the surface but coaxing a closer look. Large, mature trees line up along the cul-de-sac like graceful sentries. In late July, they bow their heads, heavy with dense green leaves. Swirly, long shadows are cast when the sun dips toward the horizon.

What was once among the toniest addresses in Dallas is now reminiscent of an aging beauty queen. As if struggling to keep its high-class status, luxury cars fill the garages, and trash bins offer a peek at an expensive shopping bag. The residents exhibit varying degrees of panache as they talk about their tickets to the opera, theater, or an NFL game. The homes, each with a different distinctive design, present a stylish upscale scene. The duplexes were especially popular with professional sports players and socialite party girls twenty years ago. But the cool kids have moved on and have been replaced by working professionals and families.

At the end of the workday, the workaholics arrive sporadically after a stop at their favorite bar. Remote controlled garage doors pop up. With sighs of resignation, well-groomed children pull their fishing poles out of the water and turn their automated miniature sailboats toward the banks of the lake. Dinner is served promptly at six. After dinner, the gates to the Shadow Canyon community close with a clang, and the neighborhood is eerily quiet on any starry night as everyone prepares to do it again tomorrow.

On this warm summer night, the stars disappeared when dark and heavy fog rolled in from one of the nearby lakes and hovered in the low-lying areas of Shadow Canyon. The cul-de-sac of Shadow Lane was wrapped in its frothy blanket just as Sofia was returning from an extended stay with her boyfriend, Nick, a stuntman in Los Angeles. Theirs was a new relationship, budding with hope and promise. She had met him just a few weeks earlier when he was running madly down a street. Alarming at first, but Sofia learned later it was part of a scene in a movie that was being filmed in Dallas.

Their relationship blossomed as hot and sticky as the Dallas summer, so she quickly accepted when he invited her to visit him in California. She spent time with him at his Malibu home to 'see where it goes.' It went south. He is now her ex-boyfriend. She gave up on him mostly because he spent too much of his time catering to his egocentric teenage daughter. She seemed to feel it was a competition between her and Sofia for his attention. The teenage daughter usually won.

The final straw for Sofia was the party at an iconic Hollywood hotel. Nick bragged about being invited. He didn't usually go to those things, but he thought Sofia would enjoy it. She was absolutely giddy with anticipation as they drove down from Malibu. She giggled and talked constantly until they arrived. At the party, Sofia received more attention than Nick did. The Hollywood crowd was enamored with her Texas accent as well as her outgoing personality. Then jealousy creeped in. Nick was not used to being upstaged. They left early and argued on the way home.

The car screeched to a stop when they reached his house. He walked in front of Sofia and unlocked the door. Inside the house, he stomped off to the bedroom and shut the door just as Sofia was about to speak to him again. She cried quietly and spent a sleepless night on the couch.

When Nick left the next morning without saying a word, she packed her bag, got a taxi, and caught a flight back to Dallas. She was not masochistic, so she could see that extending her stay would not benefit her in the long run. Even if they made up from last night's disagreement, the damage was done. She had enough self-respect to know she should not subject herself to other possible irrational criticisms by Nick.

She had learned during her visit with the stuntman that it takes more than a navy silk shirt stretched tight across well-developed pecs to make a relationship. Her disappointment at how things had unraveled clung to her just like his tight shirts clung to his chest.

Now, her mood was as murky as the fog in Shadow Canyon. It had been a long day. She sat up straight and gripped the steering wheel. Traffic on the freeways from the long-term parking lot at the airport was crazy. Her concentration on the traffic was so intense she forgot that her sunglasses were still on top of her head where she had pushed them. They certainly would not be needed in her dark and shadowy neighborhood.

She drove slowly through the fog that shrouded Shadow Lane and hoped to see the headlights of other vehicles, but she did not. She was on her own to determine where the lane lines and shoulders were on the streets that led to her house. A few porch lights were turned on and gave off glowing orbs of light suspended in mid-air. They could have been mistaken for UFOs. Her house came into view with its own lights on, as her housekeeper Florencia had left it. Her grip on the steering wheel loosened when she saw the welcoming sight of her home. She took a deep breath in and leaned forward, anxious to get into her house.

When she slid her car into the garage of her cozy home on Shadow Lane, she gave a heavy sigh of relief. She heard her little Yorkies, Truffles and Bon Bon, barking at the sound of her garage door. Like most Yorkies, they had the killer instinct, just not the size to back it up. She looked forward to the wet kisses she would receive from the dogs that were so dear to her. They never ignored her and were never in a bad mood or jealous of who got her attention. Florencia had taken care of them while she was in La La Land but had left for the night. It was a perfect opportunity to unwind and go to bed early. The drama of Los Angeles was far behind her.

The wiggling, yelping dogs knocked her over when she knelt to hug them. They were only seven pounds each, but she was too tired to struggle against them and keep her balance. It felt good to stretch out on the cool, hardwood floor of her living room. Her eyelids were heavy, and she wanted nothing more than to go to sleep. Fighting off the desire to forget everything and drift off to dreamland, she glanced around at her house. Even if it wasn't the largest or grandest on Shadow Lane, she felt the same love for it she had when she first saw it.

It was decorated to her taste with a skillful use of color. No plain white walls for Sofia. The living room was painted a dusty terra cotta shade that felt warm in any weather and any light. Original artworks were displayed in ornate frames on the walls. Collectible books were stacked on a side table, and a turntable with several record albums beside it added to the sense that a sophisticated person lived there.

Sofia lay on the floor for several minutes, allowing the dogs to crawl all over her until they settled down. Then she wearily pulled herself up and opened the back door for them. She turned the outside light on, but in the fog, it only illuminated a small area around it. She hesitated for a second, then stepped out onto her deck to watch the dogs frolic in the lush grass that covered her darkened back yard. She sat down in a lawn chair and relished the feeling of home. The wooden planks of the large deck felt warm under her feet. The little windchimes hanging from the eave of her house tinkled delightfully in what otherwise was a quiet scene. The plants and flowers in pots rustled slightly in the breeze.

She enjoyed the sensory moment before her eyes adjusted to the mistiness. When they did, she thought they must be playing tricks on her. She looked more closely at a startling sight. The eight-foot fence that separated her yard from the duplex next door was gone. Her body stiffened as a flash of insecurity and vulnerability shot through her. Her safe haven had been disturbed. Now, she felt she was exposed to anyone who wanted to come into her yard. She had been safe and content in her house for the last four years. She didn't want to think that might change with some unwelcome occupants and activity next door.

She hurried the dogs back into the house before they could wander off. Exploring the big, lumpy items she could only see in silhouette in the neighbor's yard did not seem like a good idea. She mumbled to herself and to the dogs, "I'm not going to chase you in this fog."

Since there were no lights on next door, she decided to wait until morning to ask about the fence. She took one longer look at the trees surrounding her yard, swaying a few inches in the evening breeze. If one were skittish, it would be a little spooky. But not tonight. Sofia was too happy to be home to let anything upset her. Everything but the fence was as it should be, and she felt she would get a logical explanation for that in the morning. No more drama. Her shoulders relaxed. She fully planned to take a break, a staycation.

As she turned to go into her house, she caught sight of a man in shadow. He was standing beside the duplex next door, and it appeared he was looking at her. Her body gave an involuntary shiver, and she quickly went inside and locked her door.

Little did she know the changes next door would usher in a mysterious situation to the foggy depths of Shadow Lane that she could not escape.

~

Sofia's previous neighbors, Eloise and Tom, divorced a few months ago. Eloise left Shadow Canyon and moved to a new house in a retirement community. Sofia was not sad to see her go. She bragged that she got the duplex in the divorce but didn't want to live there anymore. An upscale house in a community that had lots of single men would be her new address. Sofia grimaced at the thought of her flirting with a bunch of old men.

Eloise had met Tom while playing Texas Hold 'Em at the Senior Center, so she was hoping that maybe, just maybe, she could lay down a royal flush again. She smiled faintly and said she planned to get a breast reduction and lift, so that should help her social life. Sofia thought she was an attractive older woman who might be having difficulty accepting her age, but she sweetly wished her good luck.

Eloise had been a horrible neighbor though. She had planted a crazy assortment of things in her front yard that she thought made an English garden. They did not. Everyone who visited Sofia for the first time pointed to it and said, "What the f is that?" It was so overgrown Eloise's dogs couldn't walk through it, so she led them over after dark to poop in Sofia's yard. She thought no one would see her, but Sofia had seen it more than once when she arrived home from dinner or a meeting.

Eloise's long silver hair made her easily identifiable. It was a little creepy to see her standing motionless in the late-night shadows while she watched her dogs do their thing. There were other unpleasant events with Eloise; too many to mention. But one that stood out in Sofia's mind was when she interrupted her at a glittering art gallery opening. She complained about the leaves from Sofia's majestic oak tree falling to the ground and blowing into her English garden. She had a knack for ruining a lovely evening. Sofia explained she had no control over when the leaves fell or which way the wind blew. She didn't like to be rude, but she had heard enough from Eloise over the past four years.

From then on, Sofia looked out a window to see if Eloise was in her yard before she went out. If Eloise was there, Sofia would postpone going outside so she could avoid her. She adored Eloise's husband Tom, who was a kind Southern gentleman. His face was round and fleshy. A cardigan sweater was usually worn over his shirt, summer or winter. He would have made a nice grandpa. His life could be summed up with the fact he had served our country in the military, did not swear or smoke, and alcohol had never touched his lips. He was a prince among men.

Sofia once confided to him that she was trying to dodge Eloise. He smiled and replied, "So am I." Her heart sort of melted with empathy for him. She hoped he had fared well in the divorce.

On one sunny morning, while Tom was still living in Duplex A, Sofia woke up to voices in her front yard. Hordes of people were standing in the shade of her giant oak tree. They were frantically sorting through clothes and home accessories that had been thrown onto Tom's adjoining yard. He had quickly replaced Eloise's English garden with vibrant green grass after she moved, and everyone on the street thanked him for that. Sofia had no idea why people were now trampling across his grass and going through the things in the yard or why those things were there in the first place.

She was clued in by a neighbor who stepped away from the group to talk. Tom had rented a room to a youngish woman who had not paid her rent, and Tom had evicted her and her belongings. He was a principled man and a gentleman, but he knew when he was being lied to, and his good nature was being abused. So, she had to go. He had asked her to leave on her own, but she had dozens of excuses why each day was not the right day. His patience was finally exhausted, and he took the only avenue open to the owner. He had consulted the police to be sure he handled the eviction the right way. Such a respectable elderly gentleman; anyone would want to help Tom. The police had come to his home very early that morning and helped him carry all those things out of her room to the yard.

Sofia had seen the roommate and marveled at her brilliant red hair. She appeared to be a little too young and a little too spicy to be a companion for Tom. The eviction was executed when she missed three rent payments in a row. Sofia had never seen anything like it, but it is apparently a common practice to throw things out in the yard when there is an eviction. She wondered how all those people in Tom's yard knew there were things for the taking, and so early in the morning. She was not about to leave the security of her porch and walk across the yard to ask them. They were combative in grabbing the best clothes, lamps, dishes, and decorative items that were strewn about.

The woman renter was nowhere in sight. Sofia supposed she was either in jail or freeloading off somebody else, and she didn't care one way or the other. Her only concern was that maybe Tom had needed the income from a renter after his divorce. Income or companionship, either way, it had not worked out.

Sofia was saddened to hear just a few short weeks later that Tom had died in his sleep. Perhaps the divorce and eviction of his renter were more than his heart could bear. She wondered what would happen to the duplex now.

The answer came soon enough. After Tom passed away, Eloise allowed the brother of one of her friends to stay there. He had agreed to make repairs and take care of the lawn in return for rent-free living. Sofia had seen him a few times in his front yard but had no interest in speaking to him. He seemed to love and take good care of his plants. Apparently, his talents included being a natural at growing things. Since he was outside, tending to the foliage every day, Sofia wondered why he never seemed to go to work. Apparently, no job. She hoped he was taking good care of the duplex interior also so it would sell quickly when Eloise was ready to list it.

Sofia assumed a sale was still in her plans, as she had told her earlier when she expressed regret at letting Tom stay there. That delayed money in her pocket. She might now be relieved that without Tom, she could sell the place and move on quickly with her new life.

Sofia prayed the duplex would end up with a nice, normal family. The open space between them had given rise to thoughts of just how close the new residents would be to her, and how any unacceptable behavior would be right in her face. She could not, at that point, imagine the intertwining of lives and events that was to come.

In Sofia's opinion, caring for his front yard – it was pristine – was the best thing about the man staying in Duplex A. A frown crossed her face when she thought about the possibility of him becoming a permanent neighbor. She would prefer a professional businessman with a family, like most of her neighbors were.

The man currently staying in Duplex A did not give her that electric shock feeling she had when she first watched the stuntman's muscular physique move toward her. This guy had a slight build, didn't dress well, and didn't seem too bright, although she felt badly for assuming that. When he first moved in, he approached her as she pulled into her driveway and asked her in a real country twang if he could plug in to her electricity until his was turned on. She politely said no, but that didn't deter him. He asked everyone he saw for *something*. When Sofia had a new wood floor installed in her office, he even asked the flooring workers to borrow their saw and if he could have their leftover wood. She wondered if he had been a panhandler on a street corner before darkening Shadow Lane with his presence. Time would tell his history was much more disturbing than that.

Chapter 2 – The New Neighbors

After a good sleep that put the L. A. drama in the rear-view mirror, Sofia took her happy, tiny puppies outside. She sat on her deck with her favorite diet soda in her hand. The veil of fog that she drove through last night had lifted to reveal a clear, breezy day. With the moodiness created by the dark fog dissipated, a satisfied smile showed on her face. She embraced the breeze, closed her eyes, and tilted her face toward the sky. She luxuriated in the few minutes of sun she absorbed every day to maintain her healthy glow.

The tranquility of the moment was interrupted when the man next door came outside and trotted across her yard. Uninvited, he sat down in one of Sofia's bright yellow lawn chairs and started talking. She learned his name was Jet and wondered if it was real or made up to match his dyed jet-black hair. His face was lined with wrinkles and did not seem to be in sync with his black hair spiked up to a single point on the top of his head as the younger men were doing. Sofia thought he was probably gray and colored his hair out of vanity. He wasn't good looking nor was he bad looking. Watery blue eyes didn't blink behind dark-rimmed glasses, and a blank facial expression made Sofia look away. She held her breath when Truffles and Bon Bon ran over to sniff at his clothes, and he talked to them and petted them 'to make friends.'

After he introduced himself, he abruptly turned his head toward the duplex and yelled, "Destiny, come on out here an' say hello."

"Ok, babe. I'm coming."

A petite blond woman came out and joined them on the deck. Her outfit of short shorts and a tight t-shirt showed off her cute little figure. Curiosity showed on Sofia's face. She had never seen her before, but the fence had hidden a lot. Jet made the introductions, and Sofia wondered why this attractive woman was with him. After she opened her mouth and nonsense spilled out, Sofia decided that explained it. She was probably Jet's intellectual equal. Her conversation dispelled any initial impression of sophistication. Close up she looked much older than her clothes, hair, and energetic gait displayed at a distance. Sofia smiled sympathetically as she observed fine lines on her face that moisturizer could not erase and suggested she had had a tough life.

Jet proudly wrapped one arm around Destiny, who stood close to his chair, and explained, "Destiny's one o' the best dancers at the Men's Club. She's real popular. Yeah, all them guys would love to get their hands on her."

"Oh, Jet." Destiny feigned modesty. "It's a nice place an' the money's great. I'm makin' more money than ever before in my life. It's late hours, but Jet lets me sleep in. You'd be good at it, Sofia, an' I'm guessin' you don't have a man at home who's impatient for you to get there after work. Sometimes I wanna grab a drink an' a smoke on my way home, y'know, but Jet doesn't like me to do that. He has a jealous streak."

Sofia tried to control her reaction and tactfully replied, "Thanks for the compliment, Destiny, but I'm not much of a dancer. And I have a job I love."

She would have told them enthusiastically about her job writing for *Chocotouring* magazine. But they kept talking, showing no interest in what she had to say.

Actually, she could have easily become a dancer with her slim figure, thick auburn hair, and eyes the color of Texas bluebonnets. Contrary to what she had said, she could dance and always drew attention when she was on the dance floor. The Brazil Room in Dallas had been her favorite dance club. Now closed, it had advertised low lights, short skirts, and loud music. It lived up to its advertising, big time. She jumped in feet first on many Friday nights to shake off the seriousness of her job in I.T.

But she was not enticed by the idea of becoming an exotic dancer at the Men's Club. Her garage had a metal pole support from floor to ceiling that she joked was her stripper pole, so she didn't have to leave home to use one. But she had never tried it. If she needed exercise, stripper pole classes were not for her. Instead, she went to her trendy athletic club a few blocks from her house. It had an indoor swimming pool that she enjoyed in her tasteful one-piece bathing suit.

Destiny offered further information that she got a finder's fee for any girls she recruited to dance at the Men's Club, paid 'under the table' so no record of it and no taxes to pay. So, if Sofia changed her mind …. A frown appeared on Sofia's forehead, thinking the revelation that Destiny received a tax-free finder's fee suggested illegal dealings at the club.

Sofia briefly thought it was odd that neither Destiny nor Jet asked what her job was after she said she had a job she loved. No natural curiosity, she guessed. Instead, the conversation headed in a whole new direction when Sofia asked what had happened to the fence.

Jet's pale white stomach showed a couple of inches under his worn cotton shirt when he threw his hands up in exasperation and blurted, "I just did what Eloise told me to do. She's th' owner, ya' know, an' she told me to tear 'er down. She's gonna put up a new one an' then sell the place."

Jet thought for a minute before adding, "Yeah, Destiny's doin' real good an' we both love livin' here. Just when things were workin' out for us, Eloise says she wants to sell it. I've never lived in such a nice place an' sure wish we could stay here."

"Oh, that's too bad," Sofia sympathized, "but maybe something better will come along."

"Yeah, we had long-term plans." Destiny gave Jet a loving look. "He's a real horticulturist. He studied for six years! He's so good an' knows all the scientific names of plants. He used ta' have a great little garden. If we could stay here, he was gonna plant one in the back yard and sell some o' the stuff, 'specially the mushrooms."

"Psilocybin." Jet and Destiny laughed again, but Sofia didn't understand what was funny. She had no knowledge of the technical name for magic mushrooms. She could not have imagined the education she would eventually get.

Sofia mused about Jet's attachment to and love of the duplex that seemed genuine. While that was admirable, she still tensed up around him and could not look into his eyes. She had loved her neighborhood until now and had never thought of moving away, but if Jet and Destiny somehow became permanent, that might change. With no forewarning of what strange things were to come, she shook it off.

Her thoughts were interrupted when Jet suddenly asked her if she wanted to help pay for the fence, and she didn't hesitate to answer, "It's not mine, so no."

Destiny jumped in the conversation with another random remark, "I'm Russian. Russia has a great ballet group, but I'm not good at that. I know my strengths, an' my paychecks prove it. Jet's mom an' sister are Russian, too."

Jet explained, "My mom married a guy from here so she could get her Green Card an' become a U. S. citizen. She was one o' them hot Russian mail-order brides. But that wuz a long time ago."

Sofia knew that made Jet at least half Russian, but they didn't say that. Neither of them looked Russian to Sofia, but she supposed Russians come in all varieties, just like Americans do.

Destiny added, "My real name's Svetlana, but who ever heard of an exotic dancer named Svetlana?"

Destiny and Jet chuckled, and Sofia picked her chin up off her chest before she muttered, "I'm American."

"You know," Jet lowered his voice and looked directly at Sofia. "Me an' Destiny like everybody. If people don't bother us, we don't bother them."

There was a thinly disguised threatening aura about Jet that made Sofia edgy. She shuddered involuntarily and wondered if that was a warning. Jet then quickly moved on to the next subject and asked if Sofia had met his niece, Sundown. She had rented a room from Tom. He said Sofia would remember her because of her bright red hair. That's why they call her Sundown. It truly was the vivid red-orange color of the sunset in Texas at Magic Hour, that time of day when the sun dips down below the horizon, and its light appears warmer and softer.

As a photographer, Sofia was quite familiar with Magic Hour and had taken some fantastic photos at that time but didn't get an opportunity to say that. Jet went on to explain Sundown's mother was the friend of Eloise's who got him permission to stay in the duplex. She lives just down the street on the curve of the cul-de-sac. He thought Sofia probably knew her. But Sofia did not.

"Sundown's not a stand-up citizen like me." Jet and Destiny smiled and nodded in agreement. They were enjoying the conversation much more than Sofia was.

Sofia spoke quietly, almost as if she was only talking to herself. "So, Sundown's your niece and her mom, your sister, lives at the end of this street?"

"Yep, one big happy family!"

As Jet discussed his niece, the web of relationships among those associated with Shadow Lane came into focus for Sofia. She pictured it as a spider web and knew it might be hard for her to avoid as it was spun closer to her house. She was perplexed with this information and what it suggested for the future. Jet told her his sister's name was Lolita. No last name was offered for her, Destiny, or Jet himself. That seemed odd. Lolita, he explained, was named for some highbrow, sexy book by the same name.

Sofia knew exactly what book he was talking about. It's a legendary novel written by a Russian American novelist and has a cult-like following. It describes the kidnapping and sexual abuse of a young girl. Sofia twisted in her chair and wondered if Jet's family knew that when they named her.

The Shadow Lane Lolita was the person who had arranged for Sundown to move in with Tom and then for Jet to live in Duplex A. She was the source of Sofia's concern and what she considered to be a blight on the once-serene street. Sofia mentally reminded herself to be careful around what she imagined as a little nest of poisonous spiders crawling around the web they had spun on Shadow Lane. She did not want to become trapped in it.

Although she had lived there for four years, she had not met everyone on the other end of the cul-de-sac. She wasn't home very much, even when she wasn't traveling or working. She had an active and fulfilling life with friends that included lunches, dinners, happy hours, sporting events, and parties. Since Sundown was his niece and Jet's mother had been a mail-order bride, she could only surmise that Jet came from a family with a much different moral compass from her own.

This new information left Sofia to wonder about their effect on life on Shadow Lane and her own life, too. Her thoughts idled over a startling idea that popped into her head. There might be a negative vibe hidden in the walls of Duplex A that precipitated the events of the last few months. Eloise's English garden project that was such an eye sore, Eloise and Tom's divorce, Tom evicting Sundown, Tom passing away, and Jet and Destiny moving in were quite a lot of activity for the sleepy, leafy neighborhood of Shadow Lane.

In any case, Sofia had heard quite enough from Jet and Destiny for today. She lurched up and out of her chair, whistled for her dogs to go inside, and asked the intruders to excuse her because she had things she needed to do in the house. It was getting too hot for Truffles and Bon Bon to stay outdoors anyway. She went inside and watched Jet and Destiny step off her deck and shuffle back to their home. Her uneasiness lingered as she pondered what had shattered the tranquility of Shadow Lane. And Jet's demeanor, somehow menacing, hinted at a darkness that she could not ignore.

Chapter 3 – The Ruby Chocolate Story

Sofia put Jet and Destiny out of her mind and made a trip downtown to see Susan, her editor at *Chocotouring* magazine, just to check in after her return from L.A. She chose not to reveal all the details of her failed relationship with the stuntman. Susan didn't press for more information but made a tempting offer. She asked Sofia to travel to New Orleans and write about chocolate shops in the French Quarter. Sofia's heart leaped, and happiness flooded her veins. She loved the city and imagined how much fun it would be to go there at this time.

Normally, she would have jumped at the chance to travel to one of her favorite places. The French Quarter was always exciting with its carnival-like atmosphere on Bourbon Street. On a vacation there last year, she visited several gourmet chocolatiers who created such elaborate desserts she suspected there was some behind-the-scenes contest. She laughingly asked one chocolatier if that was true, only to be answered with a sly smile. It made for delightful chocolate shopping, but she explained to Susan that she didn't want to travel right now because there were too many things going on at home.

She didn't mention her anxiety about Jet being nearby. Nor did she express her worry about Truffles and Bon Bon getting into something harmful or maybe even deadly in his yard. She didn't describe Jet's making himself at home in her lawn chair, sitting down without asking if it was ok, and pulling his chair much too close to her for comfort. It bothered her more than perhaps it should. Even though she felt uncomfortable with the situation, she didn't want to give Jet any power over her by putting her fears into words and opening it up for discussion with friends and associates.

Susan said it was not a problem if Sofia didn't want to travel right now. Before going to California to see her boyfriend, she had taken the assignment of a seven-day cruise through the Caribbean to write about the exotic chocolates at each port. She had submitted her story with photos she had taken, and Susan was quite pleased. With that good work already turned in, Susan felt she could accommodate her on this request not to travel for a while.

She also wanted Sofia to write something she could do from home. The relatively new ruby chocolate, now referred to as the fourth chocolate, was a hot topic and begging for a story in *Chocotouring*. Sofia could do her research online and write the article at home. *What a great assignment!* Sofia agreed to write the piece and looked forward to learning more about the pretty pink confection. She had, of course, heard about it since she read every publication she could find on chocolate to keep herself up to date. Chocolate was her true love. Her previous job in I.T. was just to pay the bills.

As soon as she finished the article, she was going to ask Eloise what her plans were for her duplex. She postponed the call because she wanted to keep her mood light and positive while she was writing. But an involuntary cold chill crept up her neck when she thought about Jet. There was something menacing about him and his crooked, wicked grin and his red-rimmed pale eyes that seemed to be assessing her. He never blinked and held his gaze on her for a few seconds too long. But surely, Eloise would not have allowed him to move in if he was not of good character. She should have had enough respect for the neighborhood to keep her property in the hands of responsible tenants.

But even if Jet was a choirboy, Sofia didn't want to look at the junk piled high in his yard. There were shovels, ropes, tarps, and cans of gasoline. All that was needed to dispose of a body was on full display. Sofia admonished herself for letting her thoughts go there. Two out-of-place expensive-looking blue flowerpots completed the mess, along with who knows what else thrown in behind a lean-to. They had been out of sight before.

Now, every time her dogs went outside, they looked in that direction with curiosity on their little faces. So, she went out with them to steer them away from Jet's junkyard. All of this figured in her decision not to travel at this time. Florencia, her housekeeper, could take care of the dogs, but she didn't want her to have to chase them down in Jet's yard. It was settled. She would write a story about ruby chocolate from home and keep an eye on the neighbors at the same time.

She researched and read everything she could find on ruby chocolate. Her face showed an earnestness one might reserve for the most serious subject. She learned it was perfected by a famous Belgian chocolate company, and they hold the patent on it. All the ruby chocolate for sale was made with their product. Nuts and cream centers could be added to make a variety of candies, but if it was named ruby chocolate, it must be made from the Belgian product. So clever. It was much like the French insisting only the bubbly made from grapes in the Champagne region of France could be named champagne. She ordered an assortment of ruby chocolate bars and truffles and waited expectantly to taste them when they arrived. She was allowed to pay for them on *Chocotouring's* credit card. She loved her job!

Opulently decorated boxes and bags of ruby chocolates were delivered a few days later. Sofia looked at them lovingly and took pictures of them, arranged in pleasing, foodie ways. She looked back over the pictures to make sure they were what she wanted before she tasted them. Nobody wants a picture of ruby chocolate after a bite was taken out of it, especially in a glossy connoisseur magazine.

She sampled the solid ruby chocolate bar first so she could taste it without the addition of nuts, coconut, cream centers, or anything else. It was heavenly. Sofia had had reservations, wondering if naming it ruby chocolate was just a gimmick to sell more chocolate that had been tinted pink. But it had a distinctive taste all its own. As she held it on her tongue, there were undertones of wild berries. She supposed it was from the red cacao beans put through a special, proprietary process. The tanginess with the overtones of sweet ganache centers rested in the back of her mouth, giving a warm slightly punchy mouth taste as the chocolate melted. Perfect for when a lighter taste is needed. It should pair well with champagne. She couldn't wait to start writing about it. She set up her laptop, and the words flowed onto the screen.

Rubies for Your Taste Buds! Sofia finished her delectable article on ruby chocolate and submitted it to Susan at *Chocotouring* magazine. Her training by an award-winning chocolatier while she was in college, along with her skill set of writing and photography, radiated through her articles. She was perfect for *Chocotouring* magazine. It was easy for her to get excited about the subject, so it didn't take her long to complete the piece on ruby chocolate. She proofread it a couple of times and compared it to her outline to ensure she had included all the facts she had gathered along with the results of her own tasting.

Susan loved the article and was again impressed with Sofia's writing style and flare for the dramatic. It went far above the vanilla, chocolate, and strawberry descriptions that were so tiresome. It would be published in the next issue. An electronic payment was on its way to Sofia's bank. With a look of satisfaction on her face, Sofia texted Florencia and offered her the chocolates left over after the photos and article were completed. Florencia was an unabashed chocoholic and was thrilled to try the rubies. She would pick them up tomorrow.

"Thank you, Florencia," Sofia chuckled, "that will keep another pound off of my hips!"

Sofia kept only the ruby chocolate fudge to have on hand should any friends drop by and want to try it.

Chapter 4 – The Irish Pub and The Ex-Convict

Feeling that all was well in every other area of her life, Sofia contacted Eloise and asked about the fence replacement. She told her with no separation between their yards it created an inconvenience for her and her dogs. She knew Eloise was a dog person and thought that might inspire her to expedite the work.

Eloise assured her, "You know, Sofia, you and I have never had a problem. And this is not a problem either. I talk to my insurance guy almost every day, and he says the check will be coming for the fence replacement."

"How long will you wait for them before you just pay for one yourself?"

"Oh, Sofia, I can't pay for it." Eloise sought some pity. "I'm 66 years old, you know. I only have this new house because my son bought it for me. It's hard for me to even drive over to the duplex, and I sure can't see to drive at night."

"I understand," Sofia empathized. "But it was your decision to take the old one down before you had the means to replace it."

"I know," Eloise interrupted. "It wasn't good planning. Live and learn," she snickered.

Sofia sighed in exasperation. "Please keep me informed. I'm tired of having to watch my dogs so closely."

Eloise reiterated it should all be taken care of in a couple of weeks, but Sofia should keep a close watch on her dogs. She didn't know if Jet would like dogs in his beautiful yard or not. Sofia's temper flared at that comment. But she squeezed her fists and was able to control it, not say something she might regret later. Then Eloise asked Sofia to let her know if she saw or heard anything strange at Duplex A. She was anxious for Jet to move out. She had only let him stay there as a favor to one of her friends. It was to help him because he was just recently released from prison with no money and no job prospects.

PRISON! Sofia jerked in surprise, so much so that her laptop fell on the floor. Her mouth had again dropped to her chin, and a chill ran up her spine. An ex-convict was living right next door. She felt an urge to run and lock all her windows and doors.

"What was he in prison for?"

Eloise hesitated, then, "It was a crime of theft. I don't know any more details."

Sofia didn't believe she didn't know the details, but she didn't push it. Eloise said he was wearing an ankle monitor now so he knew not to get into any trouble, or he would be sent back to the prison in Huntsville.

Oh, that explains why Jet always wore long pants on the hot late July days when all the other neighbors were out in their shorts. Sofia retraced the things she knew about Jet, and they were beginning to make more sense. She lightly tapped her chest to relieve the tightness she felt. She had never known or even been in the presence of a convict. The ex-convict next door was terrifying when she let her thoughts wander into the land of *what if*. But rather than dwell on what might happen in the future, she decided to ask her friend from the Caribbean cruise, attorney Ryan Arnold, to look up Jet's record. Then, she would know exactly what precautions to take until he moved out.

She told herself Jet was probably not dangerous, but then again, no one goes to prison for stealing a soda or a candy bar. It must have been something big. She wondered if he had hurt anyone. She didn't think he would steal from her or hurt her. It would be stupid to incriminate himself so close to home. She remembered the old ranchers' saying that fences make good neighbors, and now she fully understood it. But then after telling herself to calm down and be kind, she considered Jet's becoming a thief might not be entirely his fault. Maybe he had been taught by his mother, the mail-order bride, to take something for nothing as a way of life. Sofia didn't have children, but if she did, she was sure she'd spend enough time with them to teach them right from wrong.

~

In the following days, it would have been impossible to tell the difference between July and August without looking at the calendar. Each day was just like the other, weatherwise, and that added to the monotony Sofia felt. August in Texas can be brutal, with unrelenting heat that follows an already long hot summer. One of Sofia's favorite poets, T. S. Eliot, and others have said April is the cruelest month. She disagrees. August is the cruelest month for her, and this year it came in with a vengeance. Temperatures seemed stuck in the upper 90s. She longed to feel the cool kiss of autumn.

    She was not alone in her efforts to keep cool. Black plastic covered Jet's windows, except for the front one facing the street. He had put a window air conditioner in that one. Sofia knew no one could live without air conditioning on these stifling days. She was not going to complain about Jet's window unit, although it was unsightly and out of place on Shadow Lane. Just like Jet himself. Shadow Canyon was still a desirable neighborhood, a respite from the burgeoning population of Dallas that surrounded it. But she wouldn't want anyone to die from a heat stroke. Secretly, she swore at Eloise for allowing Jet in her duplex, and she wished they would all run to the edge of the earth and jump off.

~

On one hot, uneventful day Greg, a neighbor down the street, skipped out of his house when he saw Sofia walking her dogs. He quickly fell into step with her, asked how she was, and how it went with the boyfriend in Los Angeles. Sofia enjoyed her close-knit neighborhood most of the time. But there were very few secrets. Everyone knew everyone else's business, seemingly up-to-the-minute.

    Sofia replied, "I need a new boyfriend."

Greg answered with a self-satisfied smile, "I know. News travels fast on Shadow Lane. I have someone in mind for you."

"Who?"

"Me!"

"I'm flattered, Greg, but I never date neighbors or co-workers. Or anyone with a net worth less than a million," Sofia laughed, "just kidding."

Greg was determined. "I'm going up to the pub our neighbor Ivan owns tonight. Want to come along?"

Sofia felt the invitation was just a friendly gesture, one neighbor to another, and it was Saturday night, so she agreed. She went home for a shower and to change clothes. It was usually three changes of clothes each day due to the heat. She was not trying to impress Greg, so she made sure not to wear anything sexy. Promptly at 7:00, he parked in front of her house, jumped out of his car, and opened the passenger door for her. He was freshly showered and shaved and wearing a white dress shirt with jeans. *Oh, no, he thinks this is a date. He's going to be disappointed.*

When they arrived at the pub, it was crowded, but they found seats at the bar. It was dark and noisy. The patrons were of various ethnicities. Big burly men made up the majority of the clientele. The décor, if one could call it that, was not attractive. It was in somber dark colors on the walls, and the bar stools were covered in cheap fake red leather. At least the smokers were relegated to the outdoor patio. Each time the patio door opened, Sofia heard loud voices and laughter and inhaled the strong smell of cigarettes. She was glad to be sitting at the end of the bar instead of in the midst of the hard-drinking crowd.

Nigel, the bartender, greeted Greg as if he were a regular there. Greg introduced Sofia, and then Nigel jubilantly said, "Guess what." His English accent was heavy, and Sofia had to admit it was quite charming in contrast to the rest of the establishment. A proper Englishman working in an Irish bar - *gotta love it.*

He said he was going to be moving into the Shadow Lane neighborhood. Greg lit up at the news and hopped off his bar stool to shake Nigel's hand.

"Congratulations! That's great. I know you'll love it there."

Sofia's eyes widened in curiosity, and she asked him where he would be living since she was not aware of any vacancies on the street.

"I met a nice guy named Jet, and he's going to rent a bedroom to me and another one to my mate, Frank."

Sofia gripped her barstool to avoid falling off. Jet, a nice guy, renting rooms? His behavior became more bizarre each day. Sofia wanted to say Jet didn't have the right to rent any rooms. Their Homeowners Association strictly forbids it. Instead, she dropped her chin into her palm as she leaned on the bar to hear the rest of the conversation with Nigel.

He motioned to a surly-looking patron on the other side of the bar. "That's my mate and your new neighbor!"

Frank nodded his head slightly but did not smile. Sofia wished she was not facing him. His gaze seemed to undress her. He and Nigel were opposites at first glance. Nigel had the fair never-seen-the-sun look of someone from England. He was attractive, smiling, and outgoing. Darkness surrounded Frank. A constant scowl and lips pressed tightly together made him unapproachable.

Nigel chattered on while he drew beers from the tap in front of Greg. Sofia fidgeted when he said Jet was renting the rooms very reasonably, so he and Frank couldn't wait to move in. Jet and Destiny would sleep on the couch in the living room, which Eloise had left behind with a few other pieces of furniture. Sofia shook her head slightly but refrained from expressing her thought, *how bohemian of them.*

She wondered if anyone had told Nigel the unit was going to be sold, and if Nigel knew Jet was an ex-con. She also wondered if he knew she would be only a few feet away as his next-door neighbor. She grasped her own hands in uneasiness and decided it was not her place to break all that news, especially on a happy Saturday night in a noisy bar frequented by mostly rough-looking men. Irish or not, they were a little intimidating since she was one of only three females in the place.

One of the men tossed a freshly picked magnolia blossom on the counter in front of Sofia as he was leaving. She looked up and saw his back as he walked away. He was enormous with arms like redwood tree trunks bulging out of his tank top. She exhaled, relieved he was too far away for her to say thank you. That might have encouraged further conversation.

She and Greg ordered beers and a snack. They discussed Jet and the soon-to-be renters. Greg didn't know any more about any of it than Sofia did. But he talked about the woman who lives in Duplex B, the other unit next to Jet. He said her name was Taylor, and she bought the place and moved in while Sofia was in L.A. She's a short, chubby, matronly type, although it's hard to guess her age.

He laughed and shook his head. "Jet told me she's 'on him,' complaining about something every day. I think she's become friends with Annalise, her closest neighbor for the last few weeks. You know Annalise will have the lowdown. She knows everything about Shadow Lane and its occupants. She follows up frequently, too, and I wonder if she keeps a spreadsheet."

Sofia kept the conversation light and impersonal at the bar as much as she could. For the most part, she enjoyed the time with Greg. They stayed a couple of hours and had a couple more beers. As they were leaving, Greg waved goodbye to Nigel, who was at the other end of the bar, serving liquor as quickly as he could. On the drive home, Greg talked about how fast his car would go because he had put a different engine in it. He punched it, and the little car was nearly airborne. Sofia was unimpressed as she endured the white-knuckle ride down the winding road to Shadow Lane at the base of a small hill.

When he stopped in front of her house, Greg leaned in toward her, "You can come over later if you want. I'm always up until 2:00. Unless you want to see my place now, you can hit me up later."

Sofia knew a booty call when she heard one, but she couldn't think of anything more unappealing at that time. She had run out of polite nods and smiles somewhere in the middle of Greg telling her about his inheritance. He was extra jovial and loud when he talked about it. He probably did it to put himself in the million dollars net worth category she had joked about earlier. But even that didn't pique her interest.

"Thanks, but I'm really tired, and I have to do some work in the morning. So, I'm going to bed. I'll talk to you soon, Greg, my friend."

Chapter 5 – The Neighbor Taylor and Her Computer

Sofia dangled her hands and rocked her shoulders to wipe off the creepiness she felt when Jet looked through binoculars in her direction. She was still wearing her favorite aqua-colored silk pajamas even though it was almost noon. She often used them as leisure wear on the weekends. Jet was in his usual wrinkled plaid shirt and jeans. His hair was tousled as if he had just gotten out of bed. He was repulsive to Sofia, even as he dropped the binoculars and waved at her. Instinctively, she pulled at her pajama shirt to make sure all the buttons were fastened. *That jerk is never ever going to get a look at me unless I'm completely covered.* She turned away from the window and picked up her phone. She wanted to contact Taylor in Duplex B and see what she knew about Jet. This set in motion a string of exasperating and sometimes frightening phone calls that would occupy Sofia's time for the next few months.

Her first call was to Annalise, a leggy former cheerleader with a TV-worthy smile and lots of extraordinary, honey-colored hair to flip around. Annalise lived right across the street. Sofia liked her and didn't mind her doing her yard work in short shorts, as some of the others did. Thankfully, they covered a bit more than the cheerleaders' shorts did. She was a high-energy, vibrant young woman, married to a somewhat older man. Her husband had been injured in a football game and had constant problems with his back. Sofia could understand if she got bored easily and used the neighborhood news and gossip to fill her time. Greg had said she was friends with Taylor. Sofia would ask if she had Taylor's phone number.

It was always entertaining to talk to Annalise. Sofia considered her a friend even though they never hung out anywhere besides the neighborhood due to Annalise being married and totally devoted to her husband. She was lively and had a great sense of humor. She had gone to college in Alabama and was known to occasionally shout, "Roll Tide!"

After some conversation about Sofia's time in L.A., Annalise was able to find Taylor's number. She added that Taylor seemed to be a nice person and had recently retired from some kind of government project. It was somewhere off the Gulf of Mexico coast of Texas, but she clammed up when asked about it. So, all the information the neighborhood had was rather vague. Annalise wondered if it was a secret marine project. Taylor had spoken to her a few times and made some bizarre remarks about Jet, but Annalise said she didn't know him. She, like almost everyone else on the street, had heard he did some jail time. Sometimes, the Shadow Lane grapevine was helpful like in this case.

Sofia wondered if Taylor knew Jet's criminal past. Probably so if everyone else did. This time, she couldn't resist indulging in the neighborhood gossip with Annalise, although it was something she usually tried to avoid like the plague.

"What sort of bizarre things has Taylor told you?"

Annalise didn't hesitate to give her the details of all she knew. Duplex A and B share a common attic space, and Taylor thinks Jet goes up there and then climbs down into her duplex when she's not home. She has discovered unusual things missing, like soda and toilet paper for sure and maybe some items of clothing. She doesn't have any jewelry or flashy accessories. She pointed out the obvious; that's not her style. So, the missing things were not of great value. She thinks Jet takes things to upset her and mess with her mind.

She's sure he knows how to bypass her alarm system since it has never gone off to alert the police, and he has never been recorded on her cameras. The only other thing she could do, in addition to the security system, was to fasten a heavy padlock to the attic opening in her back hallway.

She hoped that would put an end to her fears, but she became agitated and nearly shouted, "Criminals know how to do things, so he'll probably find another way to get into my house."

She had called the police on him three times. She told them she heard strange noises in the attic above her bedroom; footsteps pacing back and forth, heavy breathing that reminded her of her late husband, and the sound of comings and goings through Jet's front door late at night. She wondered if Destiny had 'customers' coming to their home or if there were drug deals going down.

Sofia sighed, *That didn't seem fair to Destiny. But plain women always find a way to criticize the ones with pretty privilege.*

Taylor had begun sleeping with a large knife under her pillow. Many nights, she woke up to the sounds in the attic right above her bed. She held the knife while she lay awake and broke out in a cold sweat. The sounds subsided as daylight slipped in between the gap in her bedroom curtains. She got only a few hours of sleep if she stayed in bed until noon.

According to Taylor, her electric and water bills had gone up significantly since Jet moved in next door, and she thought he had been tapping into them. The police did nothing but caution her to be careful, always alert, and call them if Jet or anyone else caused her harm. She was not appeased, so she called them several more times. Sofia worried that the police would get tired of Taylor, and if she had a real emergency, they might not come. She always felt she should do something to help in situations like this, but she didn't know what she could do about Jet. To be honest, she was a little afraid to interact with him.

Sofia told Annalise about Jet asking to connect to her electricity when he first moved in, just until his was turned on. That validated Taylor's claim that he was tampering with her electricity and water.

Annalise warned, "I'd stay away from him. And I don't know what Destiny sees in him. But I heard they went to school together, and when Destiny's husband divorced her, it was any port in a storm, and she ended up living with Jet."

Still on the phone with Sofia, Annalise described how she was recently invited into Taylor's duplex to look at the lock on her attic door. She was taken aback when she saw that Taylor had boobytrapped her windows by sticking black duct tape in an X pattern over them and had a bowl of water sitting on the floor right under each window. If anyone came in through a window, they would step in the water and that should alert Taylor they were there. She had boarded up the sliding glass door to her patio to keep anyone from breaking in there. Huge spotlights were installed on the front and back of her house that illuminated her whole yard after it got dark. Sofia had noticed that it was lit up like Vegas over there, and now she knew why.

Annalise rushed to end the phone conversation, saying she had to go. "There's a football game on TV, and you know the world stops when there's a game on. My husband doesn't want to miss one second. He likes for me to sit down and watch it with him."

"Ok, go do a cheer for him!"

Sofia and Annalise both giggled. Sofia thanked her for all the information and hung up. She didn't know what to think. Things just were not adding up. *Why would Jet, a prison parolee, break into Taylor's duplex and only take inexpensive things like soda and toilet paper? And what would he want with women's clothes?* She doubted if Taylor's clothes would be Destiny's size and style. He was an enigma in her mind. She decided to never be alone with him and hopefully never see him again after Eloise sold the place. She prayed he would be able to meet Eloise's timeline of two weeks to move out.

Now that Sofia had Taylor's phone number, she decided to call her and welcome her to the neighborhood. She did not tell her that Nigel and Frank would soon be moving in with Jet and Destiny. That would make it just one wall between her and the ex-con, exotic dancer, Irish pub bartender and his friend, who could very well have been the pub's bouncer. She didn't want to be the one to add to Taylor's level of stress.

Taylor didn't tell Sofia about her suspicion that Jet was getting into her attic, and Sofia assumed it was because they had just met. Maybe she considered Sofia a stranger. But as the conversation continued, Taylor warmed up. She told Sofia about a freakishly scary event when recently she came home from dinner with friends just after dark, which arrived late on summer nights in Texas. She turned on her TV and went to the kitchen for a bottle of cold water when she glanced into her office. Her computer was on, and she was sure she had shut it down before she left.

She walked closer to see what was displayed on the screen, and she was petrified. It was a gruesome scene of a woman who had been killed in her bed. She had apparently been stabbed to death since there was a bloody knife beside her. The bed looked eerily similar to her own. A lovely flowered pink bedspread and pillows could be seen. The body of the naked face-down woman was splayed diagonally across it. Blood pooled on the bed and floor. The woman appeared to have grayish hair like hers.

Taylor, body shaking, was frozen in place by the horror of the picture and what it hinted. But, how could Jet know she slept with a knife in her hand? The muscles in her neck and back locked up, and a cold sweat popped out on her forehead. Afraid to even touch the keys on the computer, she jerked the power cord out of the wall and the sadistic picture disappeared. She was frightened and angry.

She gulped back tears as she described what had happened and said she was sure it was Jet who had sneaked into her house and used her computer. Sofia's heart broke for Taylor. *Fortunately, one can't hear a heartbreaking like the breaking of a dish or a glass.* Not knowing how she would react, Sofia remained silent. She didn't want Taylor to think she pitied her and her existence.

Taylor continued in a shaky voice, "He's a sick and dangerous man. I've done all I can to keep him out of my house, but somehow, he gets in and does vile things like ruining my computer."

"Oh, wow, I can't even imagine what that would feel like, Taylor. I'm so sorry to hear about this. Let me know if there's ever anything I can do to help."

Taylor was so upset she got rid of the computer. She gave it to a charitable organization with a warning to have it wiped clean. Sofia knew that Taylor thought it was Jet who used the computer, but she had no way of proving it. The police would not take any action, not even question Jet. Sofia's conflicted feelings about whether she should believe Taylor or not tugged at the muscles in her face. Small worry lines appeared. *This tension is sure not good for my face. I've spent too much money getting rid of wrinkles to let Jet create new ones.*

Since Taylor gave the computer away, the phone was the only way to contact her now. She wanted Sofia to know that. After they said goodbye and hung up the phone, a shudder rippled across Sofia's body and her aqua-colored pajamas. Just thinking about Jet sitting in the dark with only the blue light glow from the computer on his face and the violence on the computer screen reflected on his glasses gave her a queasy stomach. Horrifying indeed. It would be hard to get to sleep tonight.

Chapter 6 – The Fence and Cicadas

Sofia enjoyed her morning soda on the deck a little bit less with her yard now wide open. She didn't consider Destiny to be a threat, but the things Taylor said about Jet added to her already devilish impression of him. She took a mental inventory of things on her deck each day to be sure nothing was missing. He had jokingly said he would be hopping in her hot tub soon, and she checked it each day to be sure he had not had a moonlight soak. She kept her blinds closed on the side of her house that faced Jet, but when she was outside, there was nothing to shield her from him and his gaze. Her lips puckered as she thought about how she might have to live for some time with him only a few feet away.

Two weeks came and went. Nigel and Frank moved in, each with very few belongings. Nigel appeared to be happy, almost skipping to and from his car to unload his things from a few cardboard boxes. Frank looked sullen and menacing, and his five o'clock shadow only added to his dangerous appearance. He dragged a suitcase on rollers behind him. It appeared to be his only possession. A nearby dog barked aggressively at him and the sound the rollers made on the cobblestone sidewalk. He didn't even look up.

Both Nigel and Frank wore rumpled clothing that looked like they had slept in them. In truth, they had. They were each coming out of a disastrous financial period and had been sleeping in Frank's SUV. Nigel had limited money because of the terms of his recent divorce, and Frank had been unemployed for a long time - something about a bad attitude. They had both heard about Taylor next door and told Jet she would not be a problem for them. If she did become a problem, they would take care of it. After seeing them in the light of day, Sofia understood why they were both at the Irish pub. Their appearances were not up to the standards of more high-end restaurants.

Sofia had not seen or spoken to Taylor since their initial phone conversation but wondered if she was aware she had new neighbors now. She saw Jet a few times when she was outside with her dogs. He asked a machine-gun-like barrage of questions, all with hopes of getting some money from her.

"Hey, neighbor, ya sure ya don't want ta' pay for part of the new fence? I could start on it right away."

She felt he would pocket the money and not tell Eloise about it. She just stared at him and shook her head *no*.

"Ya got any odd jobs that need to get done? I could prune yer roses for $75. I'm kinda a rose expert."

She became impatient and didn't want to see him coming across her yard or to look at the pile of junk beside his house one more time.

Looking directly at him, Sofia said decisively, "I don't need help with anything. I have a lawn service I've used for years, and that's not going to change! I really don't want you in my yard at all."

Again, Jet threw up his hands in despair, "Ok, ok, ok."

He took a step toward her in what she considered a threatening stance. Then he seemed to reconsider and turned and went back into his duplex. His pitiful-looking clothes and rumpled hair almost made Sofia sympathetic.

She exchanged texts and emails with Eloise several times, each one a little more impatient, bordering on rude. She had grown very tired of Eloise's excuses and wondered if there really was an insurance check coming. Maybe she was waiting for Sofia to become so unhappy that she agreed to pay. *Well, no such luck, Eloise.* Sofia was determined to not give her old neighbor that satisfaction.

Meanwhile, Jet continued to delight in taunting Taylor. On one occasion, when Jet finished his yard work, he picked up a pair of garden shears lying on the sidewalk. A cicada had shed its shell, which now sat precariously on one of the blades. Jet snickered. He knew that was why the shears were not taken inside. He picked them up and went to Taylor's door. She answered when he rang the doorbell.

He pointed the sharp end of the blades right at Taylor's stomach and said, "Left yer shears out on the sidewalk."

"Get that thing away from me," Taylor yelped.

"Don't like the cicada shell?"

"No, I'm not touching that! Get it off my doorstep!" Taylor's voice and face showed her disgust with Jet and the shears.

He laughed and flicked the shell off the shears with one finger. It flew into a nearby bush. Then he extended his arm, putting the shears close to Taylor again. She grabbed them and abruptly closed the door. She knew Jet had purposely left the cicada shell on the shears to scare her. She absolutely hated that man.

~

Since Sofia had been in L.A. for several weeks, she had a lot of catching up to do with friends. She kept busy with lunches and dinners with girlfriends, the raucous Missy and beautiful Carlie. Carlie's romance with a Canadian had grown colder than a winter night in Winnipeg (her words), and Missy had left her lesbian lover and was back on men. They were all just a bit off their game but commiserating with each other helped in the healing process. Sofia's experience had affected her deeply. More than she realized until she began to tell her friends about it. All three of the women were emotionally drained from their recent experiences.

Sofia assured her friends they had made the right choices, and the next romance was just around the corner. Missy and Carlie promised Sofia she would feel like her bright and sunny self soon. Her next trip to L.A. and Hollywood would be for something far more glamorous than a self-absorbed stuntman. He probably hit his head too many times to realize the prize that was right in front of him. They lifted each other up and encouraged each other to fearlessly go on. Sofia's heart was warmed by her friends, and she felt blessed to have such good ones with whom she could share anything.

With each day that passed, Sofia settled into her old lifestyle and became more and more aware she had been reckless by spending time in L.A. with a man she barely knew. It could have ended so much worse. She had not heard from Nick since she returned to Dallas and she was ok with that, happy in fact. That trip had been a waste of time, and it had taken her away from home when things were turning toward evil.

Chapter 7 – The Garage Door and Taylor's Security

Taylor woke up to the sounds of concrete being mixed and poured outside her bedroom window. It was quite dark on that side of the property, and she made a mental note to have more floodlights installed. She could see Jet's silhouette when he bent over and bobbed up and down as he mixed and poured concrete. She wondered if he buried something on the side of the driveway. It wasn't big enough to be a body, or she would have suspected that. He did this and most of his work nocturnally. She was sure that was so no one could see what he was doing, not just to escape the heat. There was no need for concrete where he put it. She wanted to tell Eloise what he had done to her property. Instead, she quickly and quietly closed the blinds and drapes on her bedroom window.

Sofia's phone rang and Taylor launched into describing what Jet was doing without even saying hello. She asked Sofia to let her know if she saw anything unusual in that area. Sofia stood with her phone in her hand, looking out the window at Duplex A. She had a strange feeling that was either fear or dread. Both were unfamiliar to her, so she stood frozen until she could sort out her thoughts. She assured Taylor that she would let her know if she saw anything, but she reminded her that she couldn't see her side of the duplex. So, unless Jet did something in his own yard, she would not know about it.

Taylor stayed close to her bedroom window, continuing to listen to Jet. Her mind raced with ideas of what he might be doing. *Maybe he's burying a small animal. Sofia better keep a close eye on Truffles and Bon Bon. Or, is he preparing a place for me?*

~

Jet didn't wait long for his next mischievous prank. Sofia thought it was mischievous; Taylor thought it psychological warfare. Acting in the dark of night again, Jet wore his tool belt, and as silent as a shadow, he rounded the corner of the duplex and slinked up to Taylor's garage door. He quietly took a screwdriver out of his belt and began to loosen the hinges. He pulled the door away from the frame just enough to be noticeable. The gap created between the door and its frame would have allowed him to squeeze inside her garage, but that was not the plan for tonight. He only wanted to let her know he was there, and whether she was home or not, he could find a way to get in. He took his keys out of his pocket and scraped them along the metal hinges as a parting act of defiance. Then he slinked back into his duplex and went to bed with a smile on his face. Destiny was not home yet from her job at the Men's Club, so no one could ever prove his successful work this evening. *So, mama, how do you like that?*

Taylor opened her garage door the next day to wheel out her trash bins for the weekly trash collection. There was a loud squeak that had not been there before. The door shuddered and refused to open more than halfway. She ducked down and was able to get outside. Incredulous at what she saw, she whimpered and held back tears. The hinges on one side of the door were loose. They were hanging out from the door they were supposed to secure. The bulb was missing from the light over the garage door, too.

She was sure Jet was to blame for both. He must have taken advantage of the dark again and removed the light bulb and garage door screws so he could wiggle inside. She didn't know what he had done or what he had taken. She became enraged as she imagined him wearing his tool belt like he actually did some work and snooping around in her garage. She grabbed a screwdriver and twisted the screws in as tightly as she could, then closed the garage door and tried to identify what might be missing. No luck. Taylor couldn't see that anything was gone or out of place, which only made her angrier.

She stormed back into the house, anxious to tell Annalise and Sofia the latest. He had the nerve to tamper with her property last night while she was sleeping in her bed. She was quite sure that was the message to her – he could vandalize her property while she slept just a few feet away. She had gone in and out of the garage yesterday with the door securely on its frame like always. It had to be his work, and it had to be done last night. Annalise and Sofia advised her not to confront Jet. Since no real harm was done, she should just ignore it. And, they said, it was possible that normal wear and tear on the garage door had loosened the screws.

Taylor stomped her feet and shouted, "Ignoring him is easier said than done," She hissed as vehemently as any cornered animal, "but I'll catch him sooner or later!"

When she calmed down, she called Sofia back and apologized for yelling into the phone. "But I'm sure it was Jet who messed with the hinges on my garage door."

Unwilling to let it go, she added, "I know people go through rental trucks to see if anything was left in them. Sometimes, a garage door opener is left. Anyone could take it and then drive around to see whose garage it opens. Or if it is a universal opener that would open any garage. But if it was someone like that, they wouldn't need to loosen the hinges. They'd just open the door and come in and take whatever they wanted. So, no, it had to be Jet."

Sofia couldn't believe the lengths of Taylor's imagination. Rental trucks, really? All she could do was say she was so sorry that Taylor was being tormented. She warned her again to keep all her doors locked and be on the lookout to see if she witnessed Jet doing something to her property.

She added, once again, "I'm here if you ever want to come over."

Taylor was touched by Sofia's kindness and asked her to come and visit with her. Sofia agreed to visit tomorrow and take her some of the wonderful ruby chocolate.

~

With a small plate of ruby chocolate fudge in hand, Sofia texted Taylor to tell her she was on her way over to visit. She quickly walked past Jet's Duplex A and knocked on the door to Duplex B. Shuffling sounds came from the other side of the door, and Sofia waited patiently for a few minutes. Taylor opened the door with a big smile on her face. She was happy to have a visitor because she rarely had one. There were not many people she would allow inside her home.

Sofia stepped inside and nearly tripped over a cinder block. Taylor had shoved it out of the way but not quite far enough. She kept it and a heavy table lodged up against her front door as protection. Sofia turned just enough to see black duct tape had been removed from the door and now dangled down on each side of it. Taylor beckoned her into the living room, and Sofia was jarred by the sight. The sliding glass door had been boarded up. Black duct tape in the shape of an X covered it, just like what had been on the front door. Cinder blocks were lined up in front of it. She supposed they would trip anyone who was able to get through the wood barricade. *This was so sad! Taylor was living like a prisoner!*

Taylor soon explained these were precautions against Jet. She went on to say she keeps all the interior doors open, even the one to the bathroom. This is in case he comes in through any window. She will hear it and see him immediately if the door to that room is open. Sofia was alarmed at her reasoning and the steps she had taken. But she said nothing. She knew any protest from her would do no good. Taylor was convinced Jet would try anything to get to her.

They sat down, and Taylor tasted the ecstasy of the ruby fudge. She offered Sofia iced tea, but Sofia said she had to get back home and rose to her feet. She was so uncomfortable in Taylor's house that she had to get out. Before she reached the door, Taylor asked her if she had bought Jet's old black pickup truck. She had seen a black pickup in Sofia's driveway. Maybe she bought it from Jet or from a dealer he might have pawned it off on?

"No, I have not bought Jet's truck. As far as I know, he still has it. There was a truck in my driveway a few days ago because the delivery man drove one. I bought new outdoor furniture and had it delivered."

The questioning was annoying. It was bad enough having the ex-con next-door. She didn't need Taylor's far-fetched suspicions directed at her.

~

When Sofia opened her own back door a few days later, still struggling with the August heat, she saw Jet in his yard, kneeling over something with his back to her. Her instinct was to shut the door and go back inside before he saw her. She was wearing cute pink shorts with lace trim and had planned to sunbathe for a while. She slapped her book in one hand against her other hand in her disgust that he was always in his yard to ruin her time outside.

She didn't have time to escape conversation with him because, to her surprise, she heard him say, while never turning to look at her, "What ya up to, neighbor?"

He sounded way too cheerful for a convicted felon. She thought he must have a super sense of hearing. She supposed he was used to listening to his surroundings while he was in prison and didn't want to think what those circumstances might have been.

He bounced up from his kneeling position and turned on his weed trimmer. He used it to cut the grass in his yard. He apparently did not have a lawn mower. Once again, Sofia felt a little bit sorry for him until the weed trimmer threw small rocks that hit her picture window. She had to yell loudly over the noise of the trimmer to tell him to stop. She appreciated that he took care of his yard, but not at the expense of breaking her windows. She was sure he would not pay for a new one, if needed. Frustration overload!

Jet turned off the weed trimmer and slammed it to the ground. It bounced back against the rubber boots he had his jeans tucked into. The handle broke under his flash of anger. He turned with clenched fists and glared at Sofia. He shouted a string of cuss words and stood glaring at her for several seconds. Then he relaxed his fists, and his body slumped in defeat. Sofia went back inside, shaken by Jet's angry outburst. She considered extending her own fence to separate her yard from Jet's. But that would be a large expense that should not be hers. She would wait for Eloise. And she would be sure to keep her cell phone in one hand at all times in case she needed to call 911.

Chapter 8 – The Robbery and The Oily Wall

Sofia had a pleasant chat with her friend from the Caribbean cruise, Ryan Arnold, a prominent Dallas Attorney. She asked about Ryan's wife, Kitty, and his sons, GOAT and Ty. Then she told him about her ex-convict neighbor. He immediately got on his computer and found Jet's numerous arrest records. Ryan sucked in his breath at the sight of his mug shot. His head hung down, his unbuttoned shirt showed thick, matted black hair on his pasty white chest, which evidently had not seen the sun for the six long years he was in prison. His face was limp and twisted as if he was totally stoned. Included on his rap sheet were theft, cocaine possession, resisting arrest, drunk driving, trespassing, and probation violations. He was a career criminal. Some of these offenses went back several years.

The most serious offense was armed robbery. He and two other men had hidden in a clothing store in a mall until it closed. Crouched down under round displays of hanging men's clothing, they were able to contain their giggles, sneezes, and burps. Jet stepped out of the hiding place long enough to grab a girl's pink tutu, pull it on over his head, and twirl around. The others who were peeking out from the round clothes rack had a hard time muffling their laughter. Jet had always had a penchant for women's flowing skirts.

Completely hidden by the hanging clothes, the would-be robbers were undetected by the teenage salesclerks closing the store. Two gum-chewing girls and one guy made plans to get out of there as quickly as possible and meet at the bar and restaurant down the street. Today was payday and they were going to treat themselves to beer and burgers before hitting the dance floor and finding a 'friend' for the evening.

Jet and his crew drilled a hole in the wall between the clothing store and the jewelry store next to it so they could crawl through. They were in the process of grabbing the most expensive jewels from a glass case when the police arrived. The delusional cat burglars didn't know there was a motion detector and silent alarm that notified the police they were there. They got away with nothing but prison sentences. Jet had to remove a lime green and black plaid shirt along with the pink tutu he had chosen from the clothing store. Damn, he really loved that shirt and felt it did great things for his black hair and blue-green eyes.

He had served six years of an eight-year sentence as a repeat offender. He got out early on probation at about the same time he moved to Shadow Lane. He had served long enough to learn some new tricks while sharing space with other convicts. He did his hard time in a Texas prison. He had a couple of minor violations since his release and that's why he was wearing an ankle monitor now. He had to check in with his probation officer every two weeks. Sofia found this reassuring - if he did it.

Ryan warned, "This is a bad guy, Sofia, and very few soften at Huntsville. You be careful and keep your distance from him. Yeah, uh, not to be one who gives up on everybody who has served time. But usually, career criminals like him are not able to kick their bad habits and rehabilitate. He did six years for armed robbery. He's probably hardened against society."

Sofia responded, "I understand what you're saying. I don't want to be unfair and judge him if he has served his time and is on the straight and narrow now. But I'm really stressed and a little bit scared by everything my neighbor Taylor says about him."

She thought for a moment and then added, "I think he can see in my windows if he's outside. But his windows are all covered up with black plastic, so I can't see anything over there. His neighbor in Duplex B says there are strange sounds at night."

Ryan suggested, "Maybe the window coverings are so he can hide. If he's hiding out, he may have committed a crime recently. I'll watch for any new police reports on him. You be careful."

They ended the conversation with Ryan, asking Sofia to call him immediately if there was any trouble. Sofia didn't feel much better than she did before the call. It was nice to know Ryan would help her, but the additional information he offered only added to her worries.

~

The neighbor, Greg, provided a brief distraction from her thoughts and concerns about Jet. Greg consistently pursued Sofia with texts, phone calls, and an occasional come-by to chat. He was not a big man, and Sofia couldn't help but laugh when he walked up with his friend's huge black Labrador. The dog was so strong and so excited that it pulled on its leash and tumbled Greg into Sofia's Chinese holly hedge. The hedge was prickly, so Sofia knew it had to hurt. He got up and dusted himself off quickly. Sofia wiped the smile off her face. Greg was an interesting guy and always sympathized with her about Jet. She enjoyed having someone to talk to, but there was no romantic spark for Sofia. She wished there was or that she would meet someone else who thrilled her.

The situation next door left her feeling vulnerable, but she was not ready to invite Greg into her life to protect her. She didn't want to react as drastically as Taylor had, calling the police at least once a week, but she knew she needed to be vigilant. Again, not to the extent that Taylor was when she sat by her front window and watched her front yard and the street for several hours each day. She had installed outdoor lights that illuminated her front and back yards like the Vegas strip. Sofia mentioned the bright lights to Greg.

He smiled and said, "Las Vegas Taylor, latest addition to crazy town."

Greg didn't think Jet would harm anyone, but their property might be another matter. He told Sofia to call him if she ever needed help. But he said he was going to sell his house soon. He wanted to move to a new location and meet some new people. He felt like Sofia did in that he would like to have a significant other but would not find one creeping around on Shadow Lane. His moving would add to the state of transition the neighborhood was in. This gave Sofia one more thing to think about. Greg gave a low laugh, raised his arms, and bent them over Sofia's head in an attempt to scare her. She laughed.

~

As August turned slowly to September and the heat lessened, Sofia breathed a little easier and spent more time outdoors. She was usually on her deck at the back of her house, reading a book or just playing with her dogs. She still didn't like being in plain view of Duplex A, but there was nothing she could do about it. She wasn't crazy about being so accessible to Taylor in Duplex B either, but she was not going to hide inside the house in this beautiful weather. Just when she thought of how she enjoyed the quiet days, another incident shrouded in mystery terrorized Taylor.

Sofia was far enough away from her that she didn't hear her scream on this particular morning. Taylor had slept in later than usual. She kept her air conditioning on so she could snuggle under a couple of blankets. It had been a comfortable night even as she grasped the knife she kept under her pillow. She rolled out of bed and padded into the kitchen with bare feet to make her morning cup of coffee when it was nearly noon. As she walked toward the front door to bring her newspaper in, she caught sight of oil dripping down her living room wall.

Of course, that ruined the morning serenity she had felt. She screamed and walked over for a closer look. She saw that the light-colored oil was running down the wall, creating a path that resembled a waterfall. But it was crooked on each side, and if Taylor moved her eyes from right to left, it straightened out. How odd! That bastard Jet was screwing with her again! She didn't know how he did this, but she chose to reject the thought that popped into her brain.

During her last eye test before getting her new glasses the ophthalmologist had said he saw the possibility of eye problems. He asked her if she ever saw straight lines go squiggly. No, that could not be happening. This was the work of Jet. Then she remembered she had suffered a slight concussion recently when she fell in the bathtub, but she just knew that was not causing any vision problems now. She also remembered that her therapist had told her to examine her choices carefully. She could always choose to be happy, but right now, her hatred of Jet overrode any other emotion. While in a fit of rage, she jumped into her house slippers and stormed out her back door.

Sofia's morning serenity was about to be interrupted, too. Jet had not crossed the yard to join her, except for that one time when she first met him and Destiny. But as she sat on the deck, she heard footsteps rustling toward her and assumed it was him. This time, it was not. She looked up from her book and saw Taylor was stomping, red-faced, in her bath robe toward her.

When she got within a couple of feet, she shouted, "Are your walls oily?!!"

Sofia should have been prepared for most anything, but she was not. She stared at Taylor for a minute until what she had asked sank in.

"Oily? You mean the inside or outside walls?"

"Inside!"

"No, Taylor. They're not oily." Impatience creeping in, "They're just like they have always been. Why do you ask?"

"My walls have oil running down them! It's like cooking oil, and I know Jet went up in the attic and dumped it out so it would leak through and run down my walls."

Sofia could not even imagine such a thing. "Oh, Taylor, that seems extreme. Are you quite sure? Maybe it's oil from something you fried on your stove."

"No, it is not! It's dripping down my living room walls. I don't cook in the living room! How else could oil run down from the attic?"

Sofia sensed there would be no reasoning with Taylor at this time. She nodded in agreement and asked if she needed help cleaning it up or if there was anything else she could do. Taylor said not unless she could get rid of Jet once and for all.

"I'd pay you or anyone else to get rid of him. With any means you choose."

Sofia didn't believe what she was hinting at, "Oh, you don't mean that, Taylor."

Taylor angrily said she did and twisted around so quickly, one of her slippers came off. Sofia stifled a laugh and watched her hobble back toward her duplex, one slipper on and one-off. Her bathrobe flapped in the breeze. She knew it wasn't funny that Taylor was suffering such unexplainable incidents, but she was at a loss of how to react or be of any comfort to her. She wondered what she would do if she were in Taylor's position. Her conclusion was she would get a big dog, a German Shepherd. That would make anyone think twice before harassing her. She was going to suggest that the next time they talked.

Unseen by Taylor and Sofia, Jet sat just inside his sliding glass door that faced Sofia's home. It was open, just a small crack, so he could hear their conversation. He nearly spit out his coffee as he laughed when Taylor made her hasty retreat to her duplex, hair standing on end, one house slipper in her hand and the other hand fighting with the wind to keep her gown and robe closed around her waist.

When Taylor re-entered her living room, the oil that had been running down the wall was gone. She reasoned with herself that it had probably been absorbed into the paint and drywall. She would wash that wall down anyway. She sat and pondered her thought process choices but was unable to convince herself there was anything wrong with her. This was all torment caused by the thief.

~

Once again, tranquility didn't last long after Taylor moved on from the oily wall incident. When Labor Day was only a few days away, the summer heat had lessened only a little. Sofia was looking forward to a holiday so she could invite friends over for an outdoor grilled lunch. She left her morning routine to place her twelve little American flags in her front yard. They looked jubilant, waving in the wind, and she liked to feel she was being patriotic.

When she drove toward her house after grocery shopping later that day, she saw that the center flag was missing. It totally ruined her display. Perhaps the wind had blown it down. She got out of her car to take a look. Amazing! There was one American flag conspicuously sticking out of the ground in the middle of Jet's front yard. It was obviously hers, and it was obviously an attempt at his sick humor. She marched through his yard, grabbed the flag, and re-posted it in its place in her yard.

It was a little thing, but she was so tired of his nonsense, that she went into her house and cried. *Why is Jet tormenting me? Am I his next victim?* She drowned her sorrows with chocolate brownie ice cream she had just bought at the grocery store. She knew from the moment she saw it that it would not last until dinner.

Chapter 9 – The Poolside Party and Halloween

As Halloween neared, Sofia didn't feel the childlike anticipation she usually had for the holiday. Dressing up in costume and attending parties were two of her most favorite things. But this year felt different. So much had happened; changing jobs, the brief relationship with Nick the stuntman, Eloise and Tom's drama, and things were still not resolved with her new neighbors next door. Jet, the ex-convict, continued to be a thorn among the roses. And poor Taylor was living a nightmare.

    Sofia wondered what would be going down next door on Halloween. She wasn't at all sure she wanted to go out and leave her house unattended this year. The black garbage bags taped over all of Jet's windows were either an attempt to keep the hot sun out or for some other nefarious reason. They could have been mistaken for Halloween decorations, except that Sofia knew they had been up for weeks previously. She scratched lightly at the mild case of hives that had broken out on her arm. Another troubling result of how much Jet had upset her.

    In the week before Halloween, it was uncharacteristically quiet, void of any action in Duplex A. That didn't last long though. Sofia's phone rang. In a hush as soft as a feather's shadow, the now familiar voice of Taylor said she thought Jet was in her house. It was very late at night. Sofia had been enjoying a restful sleep with the dogs snoring softly beside her. The little dream machine she loved was emitting sounds of ocean waves. She was not in the mood for another of Taylor's phone calls, yet she could not ignore her.

Taylor whispered, "I think he's going to kill me. I just got home from a movie, and I know he's here in my house, or he has been because the toilet seat is up. I never leave it up. That's a man thing. And I'm not entirely sure, but I think one of my kitchen knives is missing."

"Why do you think he's going to kill you?"

"It's just a feeling. He can't get rid of me any other way."

"Why don't you move out of there?"

Taylor said oh, no, she's not moving. She's not afraid of him, which seemed to contradict her actions. She asked Sofia to stay on the phone with her while she walked through her duplex to see if Jet was in fact there. Sofia waited, somewhat distressed, while Taylor walked through her home and described what she saw. Sofia's mind raced with thoughts of what she would do if Jet was in Taylor's house and if he attacked her. No sign of Jet, but Taylor was sure he had been there because she could smell his cologne in her bedroom.

Sofia asked, "Do you want to come and spend the night at my house?"

"No, thanks. He'll probably be quiet for a while. He doesn't go up into my attic until the wee hours of the morning."

Taylor and Sofia both caught their breath and agreed Taylor would be ok for the rest of the night. Sofia was wide awake now and went to her kitchen for something to drink. She jumped when she looked out her window and saw Jet standing in his shadowy yard, his gaze fixed in her direction. He must have seen her because he quickly turned and went into his duplex. There was something in his hands. Sofia couldn't be sure, but it appeared to be two cans of soda.

Shortly after that evening, Sofia noticed that Jet was now carrying a knife that hung from the belt loops on his pants. She didn't know if that was an ominous warning or if it was just a coincidence. *Was it Taylor's missing kitchen knife?* Whatever it was, she didn't like knowing he had a weapon within a split second's reach. This might be in violation of his parole agreement. He probably was not allowed to own a weapon, but was the knife a weapon or was it just for doing yard work? She again fought the urge to contact the police herself. She certainly was not going to mention it to Taylor. That would surely increase her suspicions and accusations, maybe for no reason.

~

Taylor didn't mention her missing kitchen knife again, but she continued to blow up the phone line between her and Sofia. Sometimes, the call was as mundane as asking Sofia if she would look out her window and see if there was a car in front of Jet's duplex. Yes, and yes. When she confirmed the car was there to Taylor, it seemed to make no difference. That car is there quite often, she said, but she didn't know who it belonged to.

Taylor said, "Oh, well, if they don't bother me, I won't bother them."

It sounded odd to Sofia that she used the same expression Jet had used. In any case, the car parked out in front seemed to not present any maleficent risk to either Taylor or Sofia.

~

Whether there were strange cars on the street or not, fall was in the air. The days were still quite warm, as they often were until the end of the year in Texas. Shadows had lengthened and were lacey now that some of the tree branches were bare. The breeze that swept through Sofia's yard tumbled browned leaves into small piles against her house. No doubt they would drift over to Jet's yard. Since Eloise no longer lived there, she wondered if it would be a problem for Jet. Messing up his gorgeous lawn care was not her intent.

Darkness descended on Shadow Lane much earlier than it did in summer. It was dusk when Sofia turned into the alley behind her house after running some errands on Halloween day. She had bought tons of candy in the hope that young trick-or-treaters would soon be at her door. She loved seeing the children in their costumes. It brought back wonderful memories of her childhood when she roamed the streets with her friends, feeling grown up and dangerous.

She had been invited to a costume party in the Design District near downtown Dallas that would go all night, but the host had said to please not call it a rave. Most of Sofia's friends would be there. She enjoyed dressing up and had a fabulous witch costume. She was sure, even without trying it on, that it would rest on her curves perfectly again this year. The stress of being in Los Angeles had killed her appetite and kept her weight down. She could go to the party after the trick-or-treating was done and the children had gone home to bed. It would probably just get going around 10 or 11 p.m.

Her pleasant thoughts were abruptly interrupted when her headlights shone on a man dressed in black and wearing a white hockey mask. He jumped out in front of her car and did a little, disjointed dance. Her breath caught in her throat and her heart pounded as she slammed on her brakes. It was upsetting because of the obvious intent to scare her, but also because she thought that she could have run over him. Then she realized it was Jet and her shock turned to anger. She sort of wished she *had* run over him. He, no doubt, thought he was being funny. Sofia was beyond annoyed as she honked at him, pulled into her garage, and quickly closed the garage door. She sat still in her car for a few minutes while her heartbeat returned to normal.

~

That Halloween evening, there was a beautiful harvest moon with thousands of bright white stars dancing around it. The trees that lined the street cast artful shadows that Halloween merrymakers could scurry through. The air that wafted around the neighborhood created a soft breeze that carried the smell of fall. Someone was burning wood in their fireplace. Maybe they were making s'mores since the fire wouldn't be needed for heat. It was warm enough that the trick-or-treaters would not have to cover their costumes with a coat. Parents would feel comfortable walking a few feet behind. It was a tender evening.

On Shadow Lane, the houses were decorated for Halloween and front porch lights were on. Sofia hoped Jet was not out there in his hockey mask scaring the little ones. She decided not to go to the costume party in the Design District even though she was sure it would be a ten on the social scene. Something told her not to leave Truffles and Bon Bon alone in the house. She dressed up in her witch costume, complete with a wig, tulle cape, and pointy-toed shoes to greet the trick-or-treaters. She sat in a chair on her front porch and handed out all the candy she had bought to nothing scarier than pirates and princesses.

~

Seeing the little ones trick-or-treating, she was reminded of little Harley Lexi, who stole her heart when she met her on a recent Caribbean cruise. She planned to call Harley Lexi's parents, Vivi and Colt Harris, to see how they were and ask if Harley Lexi had enjoyed Halloween. She had seen them at Ryan and Kitty Arnold's pool party shortly after the Caribbean cruise, except for Harley Lexi, who was spending the night with a girlfriend.

Sofia had invited Gabriel, a male friend, to go with her. He was an artist and art director and it showed. He was always dressed to the nines in trendy men's clothes and drove a 1957 turquoise Thunderbird convertible. He picked her up with the rag top down on the car, "topless," and they cranked the music up and felt like they were in high school again, laughing and singing. They waved at passengers in nearby cars who were either giving them disgusted looks or thumbs up.

It was a fabulous evening with dinner poolside at the Arnolds' house, good music and good conversation. GOAT, the Arnolds' son, was the singer in a band that provided the music. Their older son, Ty, shot baskets in the driveway with his friends. It seemed he never missed. Sofia relaxed into the normalcy of suburban family life. She longed to jump in the pool with its inviting, colored lights around the perimeter. It was still warm enough in late October to take a dip. She had always been a water baby and had been swimming since she was two years old. Dignity prevailed, and she stayed out of the pool, saving the T-Bird from any contact with chlorine water. She had no intention of undressing and riding home naked to save the leather seats. Gabriel had encouraged that, but again, dignity prevailed.

She and Gabe enjoyed good wine from an upstate New York winery. The Arnolds had brought it back from a recent trip and told them excitedly how lovely the vineyard was. Gabe was a terrific dancer and grabbed Sofia's hand for a cha-cha beside the pool. They were among the last to leave the party.

The ride home was just as exhilarating as the one going to the party a few hours earlier. The New York wine helped Sofia relax, feeling happy and free. She sang along with the radio and waved her arms in the air. But when they approached Shadow Lane, she felt a knot in her stomach. She was dreading what was once the best place on earth for her. She knew she was spending less and less time at home. It was avoidance of Jet and Destiny and Taylor, but it wasn't fair to Truffles and Bon Bon.

As they entered the gates to Shadow Canyon, Sofia felt the area was darker and more threatening than ever. She decided to ask Gabe to stay with her. He was more than happy to spend the night with his arms wrapped protectively around Sofia.

~

But that was then, and this is now. Sofia felt grouchy when, at midnight on Halloween, she was awakened by her phone ringing. She always kept it on her nightstand in case of a late-night emergency. She had a sense of dread when she answered, knowing it would not be a happy conversation.

She heard Annalise whisper into the phone, "Sorry if I woke you, but Taylor just called and said someone is pumping something under her house. It's vibrating the house so much that her bed's shaking. It sounds like water or some other liquid. She thinks it's Jet up to no good. I just wondered if you heard anything."

"Really? That's just too weird. Are we sure someone isn't performing an exorcism on Taylor? I've seen how that shakes the bed in movies." Giggle. "I don't hear anything, but I'll go outside and see if I hear it out there."

Annalise said, "I guess we shouldn't joke about poor Taylor and exorcism. The woman's a mess, but sincerely believes all the stuff she tells us. I'm so sorry to bother you. I know you're getting tired of Taylor, but if something did happen to her, we'd never forgive ourselves. Taylor said again since he's an ex-convict, he knows how to do all sorts of illegal things, and she's afraid to go over and knock on his door in the middle of the night."

Sofia said, "Yeah, she should not go over there in the middle of the night. Let me step out on my deck and listen."

The night breeze was balmy, and Sofia thought it was way too soothing for this kind of drama. She didn't hear anything, certainly not water being pumped under Taylor's house. It was probably a plumbing leak. But as she turned to go back inside, she caught sight of Jet sitting by his sliding glass door still wearing his hockey mask. She froze for a minute and wondered if he was looking at her, trying to scare her, or if he had just fallen asleep there. He was totally motionless, which added to the creepiness of the scene. She hurried back into her house, locked the door, and told Annalise about what she had seen.

Annalise snapped, "That does it. I'm going to call the police for Taylor. I don't want to stay up all night, worrying about her. Maybe they can figure out which one of them is the nut case."

"Sounds like a good idea. I'm going back to bed."

But Sofia was now fully awake, so she stayed up and watched out her front window until a police car pulled up in front of Taylor's duplex. Then she went back to bed, thinking Taylor would be safe now that the police had responded. She was curious to know what they found, though.

She asked Taylor the next day if she was alright. She was, but she complained about the police. They did nothing when she told them about hearing liquid being pumped under her house. She asked them if it could have something to do with Jet making drugs. They said they didn't know and couldn't do a search of his property without a reason and a warrant. They didn't hear any such noise while they were there. Taylor said she suspected Jet had stopped the process when he saw the police car. She was sure something else would happen soon.

Sofia felt depressed after that conversation. She hoped Jet would soon move out of Eloise's duplex so they could go back to life as usual. She talked to Annalise, who said she had never heard of liquid being pumped under a house. She also wondered if it was just creaky old plumbing that Taylor heard, but neither she nor Sofia wanted to tell her that. Whatever it was, they could understand Taylor thinking it was dark and sinister, especially on Halloween night.

Annalise mused, "Why don't people just smash pumpkins and throw toilet paper anymore?"

Jet was too wicked to find joy in those childish pranks.

~

Sofia picked up the newspaper the next day and saw the Design District party. It featured a picture of a statuesque woman in a Las Vegas showgirl costume with tassels hanging from each breast. Her midriff was bare and mile-long, well-shaped legs could be seen. A lascivious-looking man wearing a Dracula wig peered over her shoulder. She had won the costume contest, of course. Sofia sighed and put the paper down. Yes, she had missed a good party.

Chapter 10 – The FBI Surveillance

Vivi Harris answered her phone and had a cheerful catching-up chat with Sofia before she said Colt had something to tell her. She handed the phone to him. Colt said he had run into one of Harley Lexi's teachers who lived on the one block extension of Shadow Lane. Miss Smith, the teacher, told him about recently seeing a plain black car parked for a few hours in front of her home. She wondered why it was there so long and if there was anyone sitting inside. She got in her car and drove up beside it. A man rolled down his darkly tinted window, and Miss Smith asked if he needed help. He said he did not and flashed an FBI badge. He said he was surveilling a house in the next block and motioned toward the second building on the Shadow Lane cul-de-sac.

"Oh, my goodness," Sofia exclaimed, "that would be Jet's duplex. He's a criminal, a thief, and recently released from prison. I wonder why they're watching him now."

Colt didn't know, but Miss Smith was rattled by the experience, even more so when she saw him again parked in the alley behind her house. She wasn't sure what he could see from those locations, and she wondered if the FBI badge was real. Colt wasn't sure what this meant, but he thought he should tell Sofia about it and cautioned her to be on guard.

After they hung up, Sofia alerted Taylor with this new information. Taylor said she knew of the FBI man and car in the neighborhood on another occasion. She thinks they're watching Jet to see if he breaks the terms of his parole. Because she kept watch out of her front window, she always knew of any strange cars on the street. Now Sofia understood why Taylor had asked if she saw a car in front of Jet's duplex. Just keeping track.

Sofia had seen a man in a small silver car parked outside her own house a couple of times when she went out to get her mail. Each time, he had driven away when he saw her. She thought that was odd but didn't feel it was anything dark at the time. Now, she had to wonder. Maybe he was FBI too, or maybe it was the same FBI man in a different car. The knowledge the FBI was watching Jet disconcerted her. She again thought he must have done terrible things if they were anxious to catch him in something now and put him away again.

~

Time passed, and the changing fall weather cradled the neighborhood. There was a pleasantly tepid temperature and long, sunny days. Sofia loved this time of year and enjoyed going outside with her Yorkies. She felt much more energetic than during the extreme heat they lived through each summer. She took a few small writing jobs and looked forward to the holiday season that was rapidly approaching. She kept in touch with friends and made plans for upcoming holiday parties and other events. There is a city-wide bus tour of chocolate shops that she planned to take. She was going to pitch Susan the idea of a story she could write about the chocolate bus tour for *Chocotouring* magazine.

The neighborhood was peacefully quiet, except for Taylor and her dislike for Jet, which she expressed every chance she got. She had now begun to call Sofia directly almost every day instead of going through Annalise. They had trauma bonded.

Nigel and Frank were now included in Taylor's diatribes. Sofia still felt very uncomfortable, borderline afraid of Jet, and continued to hear Eloise's excuses for delays in replacing the fence. She said she knew she had to have it replaced to sell the duplex for top dollar. She told Sofia not to worry. It would get done. If Jet didn't move out soon, she would evict him. Sofia wasn't sure how that would work. *Can you evict someone who is not paying rent?*

She doubted there would be another pile of clothes and household belongings on the front lawn like when Sundown was evicted. Jet didn't have much, and Sofia wondered if Nigel and Frank would be thrown out, too. She never saw them, and she knew they spent most of their waking hours at the Irish pub. They might be unaware of Eloise's plans. Again, she didn't feel it was her place to tell them.

~

Shortly after Halloween, Taylor came up with a startling accusation. She felt the FBI man was a phony and was indeed a friend of Jet's. He was watching her house to let Jet know when she goes out and it's safe for him to break in. Or perhaps the phony FBI man was entering her house, too. He must get hungry and thirsty on those long stakeouts, and she has several things missing from her kitchen. Someone besides Taylor likes a cold soda.

Sofia was totally caught off-guard with this information. She felt Taylor's paranoia was growing, but she didn't know what to do about it. She was quite sure if she tried to verify their agent's existence with the FBI, they wouldn't tell her anything. And they might think she was the crazy one. So, she left it alone and continued to hope and pray Eloise would keep her word and sell Duplex A to some nice, quiet, normal person or family.

When she sat down to reflect on the neighborhood, she remembered a time when the previous occupant of Duplex B, before Taylor, had called the police to check on Tom in Duplex A. She hadn't seen him for days and became worried when he didn't answer his door. The police arrived to do a welfare check on Tom. They came to Sofia's house when Tom again didn't answer his door. They asked if she knew anything about where Tom might be. She did not, so they told her they were going to open his garage door and see if his car was there. She told him he drives a big black Cadillac. They said if the car was there, they were going to enter the duplex to check on him. Sofia asked if they were able to do that without a key or remote.

One of the two officers said, "Oh, yeah, we can open it. We have a universal opener that will open any garage door, anywhere, any time. Same for a house key."

"Good to know." Sofia was a little disturbed at this information but knew they didn't go around indiscriminately opening doors.

She then asked if they would let her know what they found out about Tom. They returned a few minutes later and said his garage was empty, but another neighbor had told them he saw Tom drive out earlier that evening.

All was well, but Sofia now had to question if the FBI man also had a universal garage door opener and had used it to enter Taylor's property. But if he was in cahoots with Jet, why had someone loosened the bolts on Taylor's garage door? They could have just used his universal remote. Another mystery.

Chapter 11 – The DPD Officer and The Pesticide

Maria, one of Sofia's best friends, was a Dallas police officer and an acupuncturist. Funny combination, but Maria worked her magic needles on Sofia's back a few times, always with good results. Sofia loved her for her bravado, which contrasts with her kindness and fun-loving nature. She was a petite, busty brunette with pillowy lips, a quick smile and quick wit. Being bi-lingual, she often broke out into a string of Spanish words when she got excited. Sofia didn't speak Spanish, but she was pretty sure most of them were swear words.

She admired anyone who could speak more than one language, and she herself had often thought of taking Spanish lessons. She was, after all, a writer and words were very important to her, but there never seemed to be enough time for the lessons.

Maria told funny little incidents at her own expense. One of Sofia's favorites was when Maria chased a female on foot after she stole something from a convenience store. She was able to catch her and tackle her.

When Maria cuffed her, the woman said, "I remember you. You arrested me last year, but you've gained weight, sista."

Maria gave her a little push towards her patrol car.

On another occasion, the Dallas PD was in desperate need of a female officer to go to Houston and fight one of theirs in a charity boxing event. Reluctantly, Maria agreed. She drove to Houston with her little cheering section, suited up in red silks and headed for the ring. She nearly fainted when she saw her opponent, a burly woman who outweighed her by at least 50 pounds.

The woman looked at her and said, "Oh, hell no. I'm not into child abuse." Her fists said otherwise. It was a short match and gave Maria new meaning to 'take one for the team.'

Sofia smiled every time she thought of Maria and was glad, of course, that she had never been hurt on the job. Maria had now been promoted to Detective after doing her time in one of the worst neighborhoods in Dallas, so she wasn't out on the street beat regularly anymore.

Sofia told her about Jet. Maria said he sounded like a real loser. He was probably one of so many they have had to release from jail with a thug-hug, good luck wishes, and a gift card for a free meal at the nearby coffee shop named Mugs for Thugs. She couldn't add much more but told Sofia to be careful. And Sofia would be getting an invitation to the DPD Christmas party this year.

"Great! I can't wait! Some of those cops really know how to dance. Do you want to go with me on the Christmas bus tour of chocolate shops this year?"

"*Si*, if I'm not working."

~

Maria returned to work and Sofia settled in for a quiet afternoon. Thunder boomed and lightning slashed a hole in the clouds on a dark and rainy fall afternoon. Truffles and Bon Bon didn't like it much, but Sofia enjoyed the occasional puddle-splashing day. She was sprawled out on her sofa with a romance novel. It was one of the few times she didn't feel guilty about being unproductive. She put on some smooth jazz music to complete the relaxing mood and looked forward to a few hours of light reading. That is, if she didn't fall asleep. She was beyond exasperated when her phone rang after only a few minutes, but she answered.

Taylor rushed into conversation with, "Sofia, can you go out and see if Jet is on my roof? I hear footsteps, and I think there must be a vent up there that he can climb through to get into my house! Will you go look? I've got to find out how he gets in here!"

Despite the desperation in Taylor's voice, Sofia said, "No. It's pouring down rain, and I am not going out in it. I can't see your roof from my house since you are on the other side of Duplex A. So, again, no, I'm not going to go out in this heavy rain, walk around to your side of the duplex, and look at your roof! If he was up there, I doubt he would stand on the roof too long. He might turn into a human lightning rod."

Taylor was not amused at the lightning rod comment and hung up as abruptly as she had started the conversation. Sofia felt bad for a second but then told herself Taylor was imagining things. She was probably hearing the rain pounding on her roof or maybe some small branches tumbling from the tree in her front yard. It could have been squirrels running for cover. There is no vent on the roof big enough for Jet to climb through.

When it quit raining and the day turned sunny again, Taylor ranted as she came out of her house to join Sofia and Annalise. They were talking and looking at tree branches downed from the storm in Sofia's front yard.

"My pesticide smells like motor oil! I think Jet came into my house and messed it up! He probably wanted me to spray motor oil on my floors and rugs." Taylor shouted, then stopped in front of them with hands on her hips.

She explained she had a gallon plastic jug of pesticide with a spray hose attached. She kept it in her garage and sprayed the perimeter of her house once a month. Since Jet knows how to get into her garage, it had to be him who put motor oil in the container. Sofia's mind raced with questions, but Annalise was the first one to speak. She asked Taylor to let her smell the container. She was going to the hardware store, and she would find that exact same brand and smell it in the store. Sofia had to look at Annalise to make sure she wasn't kidding. She was not.

Sofia's attention was drawn to a young woman walking past them on the sidewalk. It appeared she was leaving Jet's duplex, and Annalise said it was Lolita. She must have been visiting her brother. She was dating Ivan, the Irish pub owner, a reminder of the intertwining web of relationships among her neighbors. Maybe she was delivering a paycheck to Nigel.

Lolita was Sundown's mother and was pushing a young child in a stroller. Since Sundown is in her 20s, it was not clear whose baby was in the stroller. Lolita seemed too old to have a child that young. But her appearance was striking. She had black hair like Jet's that hung down to her waist. A black cat with only three legs followed behind. She was the embodiment of a paradoxical, strange, yet somehow sexy suburban mother. Her dark eyes met Sofia's, and Sofia said *hi*. Lolita smiled, and sunlight bounced off a gold tooth, but she kept walking. She wore several fringed scarves on her shoulders and at her waist. Hippie or gypsy? The writer in Sofia was intrigued. The black cat arched its back and then continued to walk just a few steps behind Lolita. It would have been a perfect scene for Halloween.

Sofia was so transfixed, she barely noticed Taylor and Annalise going in to smell the pesticide. The neighborhood was definitely changing, in transition as the real estate people say. It was getting quirkier. Jet and his acquaintances had made an impact. Sofia decided she had to get out more and see what the neighbors were doing.

Later that evening, Annalise called Sofia to tell her the pesticide in the hardware store did not smell the same as Taylor's. She thought it was very suspicious, and said Taylor is going to have a neighbor boy take hers out to the country and dump it somewhere that it would not do any harm.

"Maybe she should keep it," Sofia sort of joked. "I hear pesticide is better for self-defense than pepper spray."

All kidding aside, it was beyond unsettling to think Jet had gone into Taylor's home and tampered with her pesticide. That would be the last thing Sofia could have imagined. But Sofia does not have a criminal's mind. She began to think of confronting Jet directly to ask why he was terrorizing Taylor.

~

Now, without any pesticide of her own, Taylor greeted the exterminator she had hired. He was at her front door very quickly, as she had requested. She showed him every room in the duplex, and he assembled the chemical he would spray along the baseboard and on the floor. It would kill any and all kinds of pests. Taylor watched him do his work to make sure he got in every crack and crevice.

He told her she should leave her house for a couple of hours so she would not inhale the fumes. When the pesticide dried, it would be safe for her to return. She agreed and securely locked all the windows and doors and even jiggled the padlock on the attic opening to be sure it was still in place. She walked out of the house through the back door.

When she returned a couple of hours later, she saw footsteps in the pesticide on the living room floor, and ice surged through her veins. The footprints made a path to her front door. She had not used the front door when she left, nor had the exterminator, so there was no explanation for them being there.

"He's been in my house again!" Taylor's voice screeched through the phone. "I had a fumigator here, and he sprayed liquid pesticide on all my floors. He told me to leave the house for a couple of hours while the pesticide dried, so I walked out with him.

"When we left, we went out the back door. We didn't cross the living room floor in the front. I just came home, and the pesticide has dried, but there are footprints in the living room! Jet has been in here again! He must have come in right after we left and walked on the wet floor. I'm gonna kill him!"

Sofia didn't know what to say but wondered *what is it with you and your pesticide?* She tried to calm Taylor by saying maybe they were old footprints that rose to the top when the liquid dried. Taylor was in tears when she asked Sofia to believe her. She said Jet knows how to shut off her alarm, and he comes in and makes himself at home. She knows he's trying to drive her crazy and has threatened to call the psycho police about her. All said with a wicked smile on his face. Sofia briefly wondered who the psycho police were. Then she asked if Taylor ever saw him on her security cameras. She did not; the cameras shut off when he turned off the alarm.

"He should be back in prison!"

"I don't know what I can do to help, Taylor. But come over to my house anytime you feel scared."

"Not today. We'll see what he does next."

Chapter 12 – The Kidnapping

Thud, thud, thud on the following evening. Sofia heard the loud pounding noise coming from next-door. It was an inky night, and it was late. The heavy clouds obscured any vision more than a few feet away. Sofia could not see where the noise was coming from when she stepped outside. There was no moonlight or starlight. It was as if the moon had turned around to show her dark side.

Sofia could tell the noise was coming from Jet and Taylor's joint driveway. Jet was clever enough to work around the corner from Taylor's garage. He was in a shadow where her outdoor lights did not shine and where her outdoor security cameras could not record him.

Taylor heard the noise and dialed Sofia to tell her Jet was chipping away at the concrete he had recently poured by the back driveway. She was sure he had buried a computer thumb drive there and was now digging it up to get the blueprints of a shopping center that are on it. No doubt he was planning another robbery attempt. Six years in prison after the last one had apparently taught him nothing. She wanted Sofia to go outside and see if that was exactly what he was doing. Sofia explained she had already tried, but it was too dark on this moonless night to see anything from a distance, and she was not going to walk over there.

"How do you know it's a thumb drive, and how do you know what's on it?"

Taylor answered, "I heard him talking on his cell phone, telling someone all about it. I didn't mean to eavesdrop, but his window was open when I was working in my flower bed. I could hear everything he said. I hope they do try another robbery and get caught again. He would probably go away for a very long time. And that's what I pray for."

Delusional, paranoid, both or neither, it didn't matter. Taylor was suffering, and Sofia had no doubt that Jet was capable of harassing her. She could not see a reason he would want to, except it was a relatively easy outlet for his mean streak. There was no escape from the Jet drama. Sofia hated that she had been forced to trade the L.A. drama for Jet drama. But it did keep her mind off Nick. That was ancient history by this time.

~

Sofia became more distressed with each request from Taylor. On another rainy evening, she asked Sofia to go out to the alley and see if Jet was trying to break into her garage. Sofia wasn't happy that it had rained so much this fall. Normally, this time of year is warm and sunny as she watches the daylight hours grow shorter. She said no to Taylor. She was not going outside on a dark, rainy night to look at her garage. She told her to call the police – again – if she was truly concerned.

Taylor said there is a very nice piece of wood above the garage door that serves as a brace, and she was sure Jet wanted to steal it. He has already broken into the garage and stolen some paint. And, of course, we know about the motor oil he put in her pesticide. Sofia asked why Taylor thought Jet was breaking in and if she heard something. And why did she think he wanted the wooden brace? Taylor said she thought he was building a ladder to reach her roof more easily, and this strong piece of wood would be perfect. She often heard him sawing and hammering in his garage.

Then she added that she was going surfing. Surfing! Sofia's patience was exhausted. There is no surfing in Dallas, and Taylor did not appear to have the disposition or body of a surfer anyway. This was no longer entertaining. It was disturbing, and she had heard enough.

She interrupted Taylor to tell her she was taking the dogs and going on a little trip to the Gulf. She teased Taylor by saying she would not be surfing down there. The water would be cold this time of year. She didn't really surf anyway. She would be back in a few days. She needed to get out of this gloomy weather and soak up some Gulf of Mexico sunshine. The coast is occasionally fogged in, which delays the cruise ships that are constantly arriving and departing from Galveston Harbor. When fog shrouded the city, it was spooky, but sunshine was predicted for this weekend. Sofia wouldn't have cared. She just needed to get away.

Taylor cautioned, "Be careful while on the coast because I know from firsthand experience there are some strange things going on down there. More than what they report on the news here in north Texas. Kidnapping, robberies, and shootings by rival gangs."

Sofia promised to be careful. She would be staying at an exclusive resort in Galveston, so she felt safe. She had already thought it through and, among other things, had decided to always use valet parking so she would not have to walk alone to her car.

She called Maria to see if she could join her for a weekend at the beach. Her company would add some spark and extra security; a policewoman and her gun. Maria whined and wailed when she told Sofia she had to work all weekend and would not be able to join her for sun, surf, and sand.

"Have a margarita or two for me. I'll catch up next trip."

"Ok, I'll think about you when I'm not napping by the pool."

The weekend was quiet but just what Sofia needed to calm her nerves. The weather was still quite warm on the Texas coast. She enjoyed afternoons sunbathing by the pool or swimming a few laps and then taking the dogs for a walk. She finished each day with a gourmet meal at one of the hotel restaurants. She loved the parrot in a fancy cage in the main hallway. The parrot was a big attraction at the hotel. Everyone stopped by his cage and talked to him. He usually didn't answer, but when Sofia walked up, he distinctly said *hello* in a croaky voice. Enchanted, she answered him with *hello, how are you?*

Her room was on the 12th floor, so she could open her windows at night to a wonderful sea breeze while sleeping. She had not taken her dream machine on this trip because it wasn't needed to play the recorded sounds of ocean waves. She heard the real thing through her windows that faced the ocean. She remembered Taylor's warning when she heard news reports of gangs feuding along the border and causing trouble at some of the high-end resorts on the Mayan Riviera. But she was a long distance from those places and felt perfectly safe in the surroundings of her beach-front hotel.

She was able to completely relax poolside even though sunbathing bodies lay prone in chairs only a foot apart. There was just enough room for her to walk between them to get in the water. When she found an empty chair, the other guests talked to her and everyone else within hearing distance. She loved the friendly atmosphere, even the blaring music.

The weekend was over too quickly, and on Sunday afternoon, she said goodbye to the gracious hotel staff and headed for home. The dogs cuddled up in their beds in the back seat of her car. It was an easy five-hour drive from the coast to Dallas in the enormous state of Texas. But with each mile that brought her closer to home, her apprehension grew. She was on the lookout for Jet's black truck. Thankfully, she never saw it.

Sofia and the dogs had just entered the house when her phone rang, and she saw it was Taylor calling. She let out an audible sigh. She was disappointed that she would get no reprieve from Taylor and her distress calls, not even long enough to unpack hers and the dogs' travel bags. The dogs scampered off in search of food in their bowls and fresh water from their automatic dispensers.

Taylor rushed into the conversation, "Oh, thank goodness, you're home safe and sound. You didn't have any trouble down there on the Gulf, did you?"

The tension in Taylor's voice was palpable. Sofia softened a bit as she heard it and realized Taylor was sincere in her concern for her safety. But she was tired of letting her absurd warnings go unquestioned, so she decided to press her for an explanation on why she felt it was unsafe at the coast. She collapsed in a kitchen chair since she expected this to be a long conversation.

"No, no trouble. Why would you think I might have? Taylor, you tell me about a lot of mysterious things, but you never completely explain. So, this time, I'd like to know why you were so concerned about my safety on the Gulf coast. Do you know of some incident that put people at risk?"

Taylor began her long explanation, "Well, yes. I thought you knew. It was reported in the news, although they kept my identity secret. I thought you might recognize me from the picture. I was kidnapped while working on a government project on the coast. I was leaving work and walking to my car when drug-related gang members grabbed me and demanded one million dollars in ransom from the government. I told them I wasn't worth a million dollars to the government or anybody else. I was working on a marine life project, not building cruise missiles. (Deep breath.)

"It was terrifying. There were two of them, and they had guns in holsters slung around their necks. They kept me in a dirty, hot old shed for three days. They were disgusting, sweaty and stinky, wearing old torn clothes. At night, they got high on some kind of drugs and threatened me by telling me a person can die on just one fentanyl pill. I heard them talk about setting me on fire if they didn't get a million dollars. Then they laughed and said they might set me on fire anyway. They were going to buy hot dogs for a weenie roast.

"When they went to a nearby service station to buy gasoline, I was able to escape. They weren't too smart or maybe they were too high to think straight. They didn't tie me up, just locked the door to the room I was in. It was a rickety old shed, so I was able to knock the door down and get out. My adrenaline strength was amazing."

"Oh, Taylor, this is unbelievable!"

"Well, believe me, I've never run so fast or so far in my life! I made it out of the jungle area and saw that I was close to the parking lot where my car was. I stopped at the cashier's booth and told him to call 911 for me. It was a miracle I got away untouched by those monsters."

After a short pause, Sofia remained quiet with a twisted frown on her face. Taylor said the government never did anything about it. An FBI agent questioned her and promised to work on it, but she never heard from him again. The shack was in a jungle area, almost completely overgrown with weeds and sitting between a small grove of palm trees. The police and Federal officials asked her to take them to it, but she was not able to find it again. They dismissed the whole thing and made her feel stupid.

She has never felt safe since her kidnapping ordeal. She quit her job immediately and moved to Shadow Lane shortly thereafter. A friend had told her about the duplex for sale and had said it was in a nice, quiet, and safe neighborhood. She bought it sight unseen and moved in as quickly as she could. She only gave a Post Office box address when she left her job. They sent her final paycheck and severance pay there. That's what covered the downpayment on Duplex B. She will never forget the terror she felt while in captivity and does not want anyone else to ever experience it.

Sofia was incredulous, but the recounting of the kidnapping and the police making her feel stupid tugged at her heart. She felt great sympathy for Taylor and resolved not to dismiss her concerns or become annoyed with her anymore.

"That's an amazing and horrifying story. I can understand why you are so cautious about Jet. You're very lucky to have survived the kidnapping. Has there been any repercussion or contact from the gang since you moved to Shadow Lane?"

Taylor said there had not been any communication from anyone after the kidnapping. She tried to hide her whereabouts. She was using Taylor as her name, which was really her maiden name. No one on Shadow Lane knew her real identity, and she certainly didn't want Jet to know anything about her. It might encourage him to taunt her even more.

"Your secret's safe with me, Taylor. I'm devastated to hear what you went through. If you ever need to talk about it again, I'll be a trusted listener for you. Let me know if there's anything I can do to make you feel safer here."

After they hung up, Sofia sat down to think. She searched online for kidnappings on the Gulf coast but didn't find anything that lined up with Taylor's story. She searched with every likely search term she could think of, but there was nothing like what Taylor had told her.

In the Dallas County property owners' records, she was able to uncover Taylor's full name, June Thibadeau. That only provided verification of that part of the story and confirmed the timeline of when Taylor moved to Shadow Lane. Still, she felt a great deal of compassion for Taylor and resolved to be a little kinder to her in the future. She desperately wanted to share the kidnapping information with Annalise, but since she had told Taylor her secret was safe with her, she did not.

Chapter 13 – The Women's Clothes and The Gun Show

For the second time recently, Sofia wondered if her eyes were playing tricks on her. When she went out to get her mail, she saw an elderly lady working in Jet's yard. She was bent over, pulling weeds in a flower bed like a champ. Gray hair, a denim blouse, and a flowered full skirt comprised her outfit, complete with a straw hat and white tennis shoes with black socks. She tried to catch the woman's eye, but the busy gardener was focused entirely on the flower bed. This could be a good thing, Sofia thought that maybe Jet's mother or other relative had come by to help him with the yard.

As she turned to go back inside, she heard Jet's voice, "Howdy neighbor. What ya up to?"

Sofia's heart leaped when she looked in the direction of Jet's yard and realized it was him, dressed as an old woman. How very strange. She didn't answer him, but before she could turn her back, he stood up. He raised his skirt and swished it around like a can-can dancer, revealing his skinny white legs. Sofia was mortified, and from Jet's demonic laugh, she was sure that was his intention. To complete this stupefying scene, she saw a soda sitting on the ground close to Jet, shining like a diamond in the fall sunshine. She rushed into her house, sat down to think, and could only conclude Jet was in disguise in case the police or FBI were lurking around. And, she wondered, *Where did he get those clothes? Maybe they were Taylor's stolen items, and maybe she's not crazy after all.*

She wanted to call Taylor and ask her to identify the clothes Jet wore. After a little thought, she decided that was not a good idea. She didn't want to incite any confrontation or altercation. She sat for a long time, considering what to do. She had loved her home and her neighborhood for the past four years. But if bizarre things continued to happen, the day would come when she would want to move. If she craved danger or eccentric people, she could move to the punk rock entertainment area. She wanted peace and quiet from Shadow Lane.

Coincidence? Maybe or maybe not. The very next day, Taylor told Sofia she was upset about her socks. She buys and wears men's black socks with her tennis shoes because they stay up better on her legs. She had washed a few pairs by hand yesterday and laid them on top of the laundry room counter to dry. When she went to get them this morning, she saw that one pair was dirty, had been worn, and then put back in the exact place where she had put the clean ones to dry.

Sofia couldn't believe it. But she also didn't believe Taylor was making this up. Maybe she mistakenly put one pair of dirty socks with the clean ones. She didn't think Taylor had seen Jet dressed as a woman with tennis shoes and black socks doing his yard work with an open soda can yesterday. She asked where the laundry shelf she put the socks on was located. The garage! This was more than disturbing since Taylor suspected that Jet had broken into her garage. Sofia could not be sure the black socks Jet was wearing belonged to Taylor, so she said nothing.

~

Sofia eventually forgot about the socks and vowed to enjoy each and every day thereafter. Days in early November were almost perfect. There was a lightness in the air that one does not feel on the days of summer in the South. The temperature was quite moderate, making it easier to spend time outdoors. To fully enjoy the weather, Sofia pulled on jeans and tennis shoes and took Truffles and Bon Bon to a nearby park for some exercise. They ran, chased the ball Sofia threw, and eventually collapsed on the blanket she had spread. She gave them water and dog treats. They all rested and watched the gray and white clouds perform slow-motion somersaults across the sky. Then Sofia clipped their leashes back on the dog's collars and led them to the car in the parking lot. As she opened the back door of her car, a black pickup truck stopped behind her. The driver rolled down the window, and Sofia was astounded to see it was Jet.

He said, "Ya got any o'that pink chocolate, neighbor? Give my love to your dogs."

Then he laughed and drove away. *Has he followed me to the park*, she wondered. *And how did he know about the ruby chocolate? Was it possible he had seen my story about it on my computer?* Taylor had hinted that he broke into her duplex and used her computer. Sofia doubted he was a subscriber to *Chocotouring* magazine, the only place her article on ruby chocolate had been published for public consumption. *How else could he know?* Sofia's hands shook as she drove home. *Why is Jet taunting me?* Thoughts about Jet swirled in her head but did not collide to result in a resolution.

She devised a plan to find some answers. There was ruby chocolate fudge in her freezer that she had kept for herself instead of giving it to Florencia. She thawed it and cut it into small pieces, then put it on a plate and took it with her and her soda to her favorite spot on the deck. She sat in the shaded area so the chocolate wouldn't melt but made sure it was in Jet's line of view. She would not be intimidated by him. She thought the plate of ruby chocolate might draw him out, and she was going to ask him how he knew about it.

The plan worked. Soon, Jet and Destiny walked across her yard to join her on the deck. Sofia greeted them and offered them a piece of fudge. They both accepted and moaned at the deliciousness of the candy. Then Sofia asked pointedly what Jet was doing at the park and how he knew about the pink chocolate.

Destiny looked at Jet as one would look at an unruly child, "I told ya not to do that."

She turned her head to speak to Sofia and blurted out, "Jet saw your delivery man th' other day an' rushed out there to see what you wuz gettin'. He read the words 'Ruby Chocolate' on the box and looked it up on th' internet. He's so nosey! He can get th' internet on his phone. Not like Taylor who says she doesn't have a computer. She said it was just one more thing that might get stolen from her. And she doesn't know how t' get th' internet on her phone."

"Oh, I see. Well, that's one mystery solved. I didn't think anyone knew I had ruby chocolate at my house."

Sofia felt somewhat relieved and wondered if there was a logical explanation for all the things Taylor had described. Jet might be toying with her to satisfy some warped sense of humor or Taylor might be paranoid and imagining things after her kidnapping experience. Or there might be a negative vibe at the duplexes next door that causes everyone to behave abnormally. Sofia's body was frozen in uncertainty.

~

A few days later, on a perfect fall evening, Taylor stepped out onto her brick-covered courtyard to look at the brilliantly colored sunset on full display in the West. She didn't have trees in her back yard to block the view, so she was soaking it in. She was smiling and relaxing until she heard someone digging near her side yard. She didn't even have to look. She knew it was Jet, and she was furious once again. *Why can't that man just sit still?* There had been a terrible smell coming from Jet's duplex earlier that day, and she wondered if he was now burying a decaying dead body. She immediately picked up the phone to tell Sofia about it.

Sofia let out a little yelp when Taylor speculated about Jet burying a dead body. She told Taylor not to go outside to look and put herself in any danger. She reasoned that being a thief is a long way from being a killer, but Taylor had heard Jet beating Destiny and said it was possible he had gone too far this time.

Sofia asked, "Have you seen Destiny today?"

"No, not today. Who can we get to go outside and see what he's doing? I know, I'll ask Annalise."

She seemed more concerned about the noise than about Destiny and made a call to Annalise. She declined the invitation to walk over to Taylor's duplex and see what was going on. She and Sofia were both exhausted by Taylor's never-ending dialogue. Sofia was just about ready to pack her bags and move. She thought perhaps Taylor didn't like Jet and wanted to frame him for something. Whatever her motivation was, she had made the neighborhood less enjoyable. She had cried wolf so many times that Sofia and Annalise were finding it easier to ignore her. That was their reaction this time. They never did find out if Jet or anyone else was digging a hole that evening. They had no interest or energy for checking it out later.

Taylor retired to her bedroom again with her knife in one hand and her cell phone in the other. She prayed for a quiet night in the attic and a good sleep for herself. But it was hard for her to even close her eyes. She was constantly tired and haggard looking these days due to the lack of sleep. She wanted someone to help her, but she had no one to turn to except Sofia and Annalise. Neither of them was large or muscular, so she knew they couldn't help in any physical altercation even if they tried. She cried about it often.

~

When Taylor returned home from church on Sunday morning, she felt calm, almost serene, as she always did after a church service. She needed to hear the Good Word once a week to strengthen her against whatever the following days held. She especially enjoyed the music and fancied herself a pretty good singer. She pulled into her garage, humming, and was thankful there appeared to be no new signs of Jet having been there. She walked happily through the adjoining door that took her into her kitchen. She locked the three locks on the door behind her. When she stepped into her kitchen, she stopped dead still in her tracks while her breath caught in her throat. There were dirty pans and dishes in her sink.

The sink had been empty when she left for church just two hours ago. She twirled around quickly to make sure Jet was not standing right behind her. She went room by room, looking in closets and under beds. Her heart was racing from fear and anger. Jet wasn't there, but this was the last straw. If she couldn't feel safe leaving her home to go to church, it was time for her to take action.

It had been in the back of her mind for a while, and now it was front and center – she was going to buy a gun. A small gun would give her peace of mind, and she would hope she never had to use it. After making this decision, she punched number one on her speed dial to tell Sofia what Jet had done. Still in a church-state of mind, she hoped the Lord had seen him.

Taylor hissed, "Jet came in my house and used some pans and dishes. He cooked something, probably sat himself down at my table, and ate. I suppose he ate my food, but I haven't checked the refrigerator yet. It smells like bacon and eggs in here. Then he put the dirty dishes in my sink!

"If you don't believe me, come over and look at the pans in my sink. I'm going to throw them away. I don't want to touch anything he's touched. He probably coated them with poison anyway! You know if anything happens to me, Jet is to blame!"

Sofia told her it would not be necessary for her to come and look in her sink. She believed that Taylor *thought* Jet had used her pots and pans. She didn't say it, but she knew looking at dirty pans in the sink would in no way prove to her who used them.

Taylor replied with a "hmmmpf!"

She looked in her mirror and saw that her face was tense and drawn. She had wrinkles and no longer resembled the perky young woman she thought she still was. What she didn't know was that she reminded Jet of his mother, and that was the source of his desire to torment her. Taylor resembled his mother physically. Her voice, except for the Louisiana accent, could have been his mother's – scolding him for something he didn't even know he had done. He despised Taylor for her stability and owning her home. And she had a never-ending supply of soda! Whether or not Jet understood the source of his resentment is not clear. His thoughts were about what he would do next and how far he could take this without winding up back in prison for something more serious than theft.

~

The TV commercial she had seen about the gun show had not prepared Taylor for the enormity of the event. She had driven out in the country to a ranch, the home of the wildly popular TV show in the 1980s. The familiar white ranch-style house did not come into view for a while because of all the traffic backed up on the road in front of it. Taylor smiled when she finally saw it. She had loved that show.

The commercial for the gun sale had said it would feature dozens of vendors, but Taylor was not expecting so many people to attend. It was a traffic nightmare, but she finally found a parking spot.

She walked the length of a football field to reach the sale inside a large tent on the grounds.

There was every sort of human being possible in attendance. There were weathered cowboys, rodeo gals, punky-looking young people, conservative ones like herself, and a few that looked like absolute asylum escapees. She was especially taken with an elderly man dressed in shorts made from fabric in the pattern of the American flag. He sported a foot-long gray beard, cowboy boots with spurs that jingled, and a large Old Glory in his hand as he rode by on a motorized scooter. *But, hey, this is Texas, a big state with enough room for everyone.*

Taylor paid $10.00 for admission and stopped to read the large sign by the door:

1. No loaded open or concealed carrying of firearms
2. No loose ammunition
3. No photography
4. No alcohol, drugs or controlled substances
5. No vulgar or profane behavior or attire

Taylor had no problem with any of the rules and stepped into the swarm of people gathered at each vendor's counter. She wanted to see everything so she could make the best decision on her handgun purchase. It was exhilarating to be part of such a diverse and energetic crowd. She wished she had not worn her tweed blazer and gabardine pants. Jeans and a cotton shirt would have been more appropriate. She was afraid others would think she didn't belong there.

Thousands of gleaming firearms were on display. They filled glass cases and shelves on the walls. Taylor didn't know where to start, so she just blended in and went with a group of people as they moved from one counter to another. After browsing around for nearly an hour, her feet hurt, and she decided not to pay the exorbitant prices posted for small guns. She would ask for advice from a gun dealer but thought she would be most comfortable with a 22-caliber pistol. She began to feel claustrophobic and a little disoriented, so she left without a gun but with the intention of visiting a smaller, local gun shop in Dallas in the next few days.

Chapter 14 – The Honky Tonk and The Flowerpots

The music stopped, and the lights came on in a south Dallas honky-tonk. Three couples on the dance floor who had swayed like the flickering flames of a candle looked up in surprise. They separated and slowly left the dance floor to grab their coats and prepare to leave. A waitress who looked as tired as the old green carpet under her feet cleared away glasses and dishes.

As she approached her last table, she said, "Wake up, cowboy! We're closing."

The lights and sound of silence were enough for Jet to lift his head and squint at her. "What time is it?"

"It's 2 a.m., closing time."

"Aw, ok."

Jet struggled to his feet and walked shakily to the exit. He stopped and held onto the door frame to regain his balance while an inebriated couple nearly fell out the door ahead of him.

A large man, the bouncer, who was dressed in full-on cowboy gear from hat to belt buckle to boots, said, "Come on, y'all. This way and be careful out there on the road."

The last few cars left the parking lot as Jet zigzagged his way to his truck. He climbed in and shook his head to clear it enough to decide which way was home. He drove a few blocks north, he thought, but felt dizzy and drowsy. Deciding to play it safe, he pulled into a large parking lot on his right side because he knew Destiny would have a hissy fit if he wrecked his pickup again. It seemed the best thing would be to park under one of the huge lights in the parking lot and sleep it off.

There was a car, a motor home, and two pick-up trucks in the parking lot. It was well known that this big-box retailer would allow people to park there overnight, so Jet joined the group. He turned off the engine and locked the doors to his pickup before immediately passing out in the driver's seat. His head fell back against the headrest, and he began to snore.

They say the only people awake at 3 a.m. are the lonely and the loved. Jet was neither, but he sat up straight when he awoke and looked at the clock. He'd better get home. Destiny would be there already after her shift at the Men's Club. If she had a rough night, she might already be asleep, and he could avoid another argument and questions about where he had been and why he couldn't get a job. He had done a couple of handyman jobs for a guy he knew from Huntsville; made fifty bucks. Then they went to the boot scootin' bar where he woke up alone at closing time. He spent all of the fifty bucks. He gave the waitress a nice tip so she'd know he's no deadbeat.

Interesting code of conduct for a convicted thief. He hadn't done anything wrong tonight, except the terms of his parole said he was not to socialize with other felons. *Well, screw that,* he thought, *I'll pick my own friends.* It was a chilly evening, but the beer had warmed him up. He didn't need his coat that lay on the seat beside him. *Coats are for sissies.* He had recently had his ankle monitor removed, and the stop at the honky-tonk was a celebration of that. He was feeling pretty good about himself.

He drove out of the parking lot and headed north, toward home again, he thought. He tried to drive slowly and steadily, but the truck seemed like it had a mind of its own. He could hear the little lane markers under his tires and feel the bumps when he wandered over them. Even in his mentally compromised state, he sensed there was a car following him. He liked to think he had the cat-like senses of a master thief. After a couple more swerves from lane to lane, the lights on top of the cop car behind him lit up, and a siren screamed. Jet sighed in resignation, pulled over to the side of the street and stopped. His life had been full of police officers, so he wasn't too uncomfortable about talking to one. Especially when he was still slightly buzzed from the alcohol. The officer who came up to his side window was one of those formidable-looking Texans. He was tall and muscular, mustache, hat, crisp uniform, suntan, shiny wristwatch, and deep, gravelly voice – Destiny would have loved him.

The cop shined his flashlight on Jet's face and immediately told him to get out of the truck. The next steps of police protocol followed, and when Jet could not walk a straight line, he was loaded into the back seat of the patrol car. His heavy eyelids drooped and the next thing he remembered was the clink of the lock on his cell.

He muttered to himself, "Three squares a day, a bed, and a roof over my head. Jail ain't so bad."

During his stay at county jail, Jet had plenty of time to think. Old memories flooded in when least wanted. He thought a lot about his mother, the hot Russian mail order bride who ended up bored, lonely, and overweight before she died. He never forgave her for her decline. It was embarrassing. She became a metaphor for most everything in his life. Things started out warm and hopeful and ended in despair. She hadn't been much of a mother in the traditional American sense. Not cruel exactly, but not warm and loving either. Jet's resentment for her grew with each soda she drank in front of him while forbidding him to have one.

~

There were unusually quiet days on Shadow Lane while Jet sobered up in the county jail. Sofia could have asked Taylor about Jet and Destiny, but she was so happy with the peaceful interlude, she didn't want to stir things up. Eventually, Taylor took the initiative and seemed to gloat as she told her Jet was back in jail. He had been arrested for drunk driving. Eloise, the absentee owner of Duplex A, had told Taylor that she had heard from her friend Lolita that Jet was in jail. The grapevine was intact. She asked if Taylor could keep an eye on the place while he was away.

Taylor spilled the beans about the other two men, Nigel and Frank, living there, and asked exactly what she should be keeping an eye on. Eloise had not known about the two extra renters in her property. Jet had charged each of them two months' rent in advance and had pocketed the money himself, which he spent immediately on marijuana. Instead of giving Nigel and Frank's rent money to Eloise he got some really good weed but told Destiny he would find a way to grow his own. That was unethical on so many levels. Eloise said she hoped the duplex would be sold in less than a month, and she certainly was not going to refund their rent.

~

Taylor was up bright and early and was feeling happy that Jet was in jail. He had been there for a while, and she hoped he stayed forever. It was quite relaxing not thinking about what devious prank he would pull off next. She had a few nights of uninterrupted sleep with no sounds in her attic. She sailed through her duplex, making sure everything was in its place. Then she rolled the large, heavy dresser away from the front door where she had placed it every night. It was there to block Jet if he tried to come in the traditional way, rather than through the roof or attic.

She pulled the curtains open on the window beside the front door and gasped as she jumped backward. She tripped over the cinder block nearby and rolled onto the floor. There he was, standing outside her front window on the small sidewalk that led up to it. He was just about to ring her doorbell when he saw her through the window and grinned like a monkey.

"Open th' door, Taylor. I wanna give ya' some flowerpots."

Taylor picked herself up and opened the door. Jet told her he had just finished serving his time for a DUI and had been told by Eloise that the duplex was sold. He and his renters would have to move out within one week. He wouldn't be able to take everything he had so he wanted to give the two vivid blue flowerpots to Taylor.

"Why, thank you. That's very nice, and yes, I'd love to have them."

Jet went to his side yard and then returned to Taylor with the flowerpots in hand. They were about 24 inches tall and in a bright shade of Mediterranean blue.

He set them down on the sidewalk and said, "I'll give 'em to you for $50 each."

He was under the impression that Taylor had a lot of money.

Taylor was flabbergasted. When he said he wanted to give them to her, he didn't say anything about charging money for them. Typical Jet - always on the hustle, always a little dishonest.

"No, thank you. I didn't know you were going to charge me for them. I don't really need them, so you can take them back."

"Aw, come on. Ya' need these. They'll look good on yer patio an' then I can climb on 'em to get on your roof." His smirk was sickening. This was his idea of a joke, but it was not funny to Taylor.

She slammed the door shut and closed the curtains. Her day had been ruined and it wasn't even noon yet. On the bright side, she knew Jet would soon find out Destiny had moved and was staying with a man she met at the Men's Club. That would have to be hard on Jet's inflated male ego.

As fate would have it, Sofia was in her front yard and heard the conversation between Jet and Taylor. She hoped to get back inside before Jet saw her, but by the time she had shut off her sprinkler system, Jet was standing way too close. He asked her if she wanted to buy the flowerpots, and she said no thanks. He put them down on his lawn and started walking toward a beat-up bicycle parked on the sidewalk. He grabbed the backpack on the fender of the bike and put it on, along with some goggles. He smiled and told Sofia someone had taken his truck, so he was bulking up his quadriceps by bike riding. *Yeah, right.* Sofia felt sure his truck had been impounded after his DUI. Maybe he didn't have the money to get it out. He looked like an absolute idiot in the goggles, pants legs rolled up, and hair a windblown mess.

Looking back over his shoulder as he pedaled off, "I'm gonna be movin' out o' here soon. But I'll miss Taylor and you, an' I'll have to come back an' visit."

"Oh, great."

~

Enjoying temporary relief from Taylor, Jet, and his bicycle, Sofia was in a restaurant having dinner with friends. She did not answer her phone when she saw that Taylor was calling. She didn't feel like diving into her negativity while she was having a great time with Missy and Carlie. Instead, she raised her wine glass and facetiously toasted, "Here's to good neighbors."

Carlie and Missy laughed and said, "Don't answer it," when Taylor immediately called back again.

"Might as well get it over with or she will keep calling. But I'm seriously thinking about telling her not to ever call me again."

Taylor shouted into the phone that she had just returned home, and when she opened her garage door, there was a can of antifreeze sitting in the middle of the floor.

"I think that's a warning from him - Jet! I think he's going to poison me!"

"Why do you think that?"

"Why else would he break in and leave antifreeze on the floor? Everyone knows it's hard to detect it when someone drinks it. It's been used in a lot of crimes I've seen on TV."

Sofia took a minute to think before replying, "This is getting into some serious accusations, Taylor. If you really believe that, maybe you should hire a security guard or move out."

"Oh, no. He doesn't scare me. I'll catch him! Goodbye."

Sofia signaled the waiter for another bottle of Pinot for the table. She was in no hurry to get home. Missy was ready to go clubbing and see what single men were out on the town tonight. Why not, agreed Sofia and Carlie.

~

After Taylor got no help in looking for Jet to see if he was breaking into her garage or digging in her yard, she was feeling anxious for someone to listen to her and validate her. No one had said they didn't believe her, but she sensed some hesitation when she described Jet's actions to Sofia and Annalise. The next time, she was going to give details and take pictures.

When she went outdoors to her backyard to water some plants, she saw a hole cut in her gate. She walked over to it for a closer inspection. It was roughly cut and about the size of a tennis ball. It had not been there before. Taylor had excellent eyesight and attention to detail. She was positive Jet had drilled this hole so he could spy on whatever was in her backyard.

She marched back inside and grabbed her Polaroid camera (still didn't know how to use all the features of her cell phone). She took pictures of the hole. She wished she had a picture of how it looked before, but she felt this would provide proof of what a destructive monster Jet was. She found a dirty sock in her garage laundry area and nailed it over the hole in the gate. *Stick your nose into that, Jet!*

Chapter 15 – The Chocolate Tour and The Mushrooms

There was a chill in the air when the calendar pages turned to November. Trees were bare, and the fallen leaves had blown into small piles in sheltered areas. When the wind swept over the branches stripped of all their color, they swayed and jabbed like a prize fighter. The shadows splayed on the ground were spindly and more closely resembled the fingers of an arthritic spinster than a fighter. Sofia didn't care much for winter and cold weather, but she reminded herself the holidays would take her mind off it. There were several things coming up to keep her busy, and she was enjoying being fancy-free with no man in her life to consider.

"It's not too soon to start Christmas shopping, is it?" Sofia talked to Maria about the chocolate shop bus tour and said they should go ahead and get tickets because she planned to pre-order chocolate gifts for Christmas presents this year. They agreed on a date and bought tickets.

The day of the tour, they met in a parking lot in north Dallas, where the bus awaited them and 22 other guests. Sofia instinctively looked around the parking lot before climbing up the steps to the bus. Her body jerked, and her head twisted to one side. There was a black pickup truck parked close to her car. She felt momentary anger. But it couldn't be Jet. His truck might still be at the city impound lot after his drunk driving incident. She wasn't sure. It was 8 a.m. on a Saturday morning. Surely, he wouldn't get up early just to follow her. She was holding up the traffic of the others who were lined up to climb onto the bus. She turned and rushed up the steps without another look back. The sight of the black truck would haunt her all day.

They were greeted with little individual bottles of wine when they boarded the luxurious bus. It was a very festive atmosphere as they sunk into their comfortable seats and looked out through curtained bus windows. The black truck was gone, and Sofia breathed a sigh of relief.

She told Maria about seeing the truck. Maria agreed that would be worrisome, but no laws were broken. She couldn't do anything, especially since the truck was now gone. It was good for Sofia to be aware of her surroundings as long as it didn't infringe on her normal life. Maria, as a rookie detective, had been assigned to an area nobody on the force wanted. Since they were in north Dallas, it was not her beat – another reason for her to hesitate to take any action, or she might have approached him and questioned him. She pulled her jacket open enough to show Sofia her gun was holstered on her side.

She patted Sofia's hand. "We're all right, but if you want to get a gun of your own, I'll help you. And I can go with you for shooting lessons. You might as well. Most everyone in Texas has a gun."

"I'll think about it."

"Ok, let's forget it for now and put Jet and the black truck out of our minds. Just enjoy the day."

They turned their attention to the tour hostess on the bus, who was terrific. She was very animated and upbeat in her presentation. She announced there would be four stops on the tour: three chocolate shops and one cake bar. Lunch would be served at the second location. She would be asking trivia questions and presenting the winners with chocolates.

As the bus rolled onto the North Dallas Tollway, heading downtown, the driver broke out into song. The ladies on the bus became quiet while he sang. He had a deep, rich voice and delivered a classic Christmas carol flawlessly. It was an unexpected bonus to the bus tour.

The first stop was in a trendy shopping area in south Dallas. The local chocolate shop was quirky, with tons of confections from which to choose. The owner, who had lots of impressive credentials, came out of the kitchen to greet them. She was tattooed from knuckles to neck. A perfect fit with the area and vibe of her shop.

    There were samples of six different chocolates, all to die for. Sofia was thrilled with the creative names and descriptions, the most unusual of all – the Wham Wham Bar, made with "matcha and candied Japanese breadcrumbs added to white chocolate." Most of the bus tourists bought things, and Sofia ordered unique, liquor-flavored chocolates for her Christmas gift list.

    A large statue of a rock and roll legend looked down on the festivities from the highest shelf. He had a smile on his face, which seemed to say he approved of all that was going on down below. The bus took the long way out of the area so the tour guide could point out the building where Bonnie and Clyde were known to hang out. It was now home to a restaurant-flower shop combination.

    The second stop was for lunch at a café and chocolate shop near downtown. Most chocolate shops double as something else, like a flower shop, gift shop, or café. Sofia assumed selling only chocolates didn't pay the rent. The food was good, and the glass case of chocolates was immense. Sofia and Maria sat at a table with two other ladies and soon became friends. They loved the soup and sandwiches. Each of them bought one truffle to eat as their dessert.

    The third stop was at the sleek, modern shop, owned by the bouncy blond namesake of the store. The shop was in the Trinity Groves area at the foot of the iconic Santiago Calatrava bridge with its brilliant white beams. It was almost blinding in the sunlight over the Trinity River. A landmark no one could miss. Sofia ordered a few boxes of caramel-filled chocolate Christmas trees and knew she would have to hide them if they were to last until Christmas.

    While walking across the parking lot to get back on the bus, someone tapped her on the shoulder. She turned and nearly fainted when she saw it was Jet. "Howdy, neighbor. I guess I'm not the only one that likes candy."

    Before Sofia could recover from the shock, he turned and galloped off to the other side of the building where his truck was parked. Maria had guessed who he was, "That guy's a creep! And it sure seems like he's stalking you. I'm going to see if I can get someone on the force to watch him."

Sofia was shaking, "I want to scream. He's so sneaky. He just appears out of nowhere. I think he knows I hate him, so why the charade of being nice to me?"

Maria explained that's what criminals do, hoping you'll let your guard down. So, "Don't. Be aware of your surroundings and let me know if he causes any real trouble."

The final stop on the chocolate tour was at a cake shop, an absolute delight for the senses. The aroma of freshly baked cakes was seductive. Intricately decorated cakes were on display, and three different cake flavors were sampled.

Chocolate, of course, was the first to be tasted since this was a chocolate tour. It was a four-layer "super-rich and moist chocolate cake with dark chocolate frosting." Hummingbird cake, "a true Southern classic moist cake with toasted pecans, pineapple, banana and a hint of cinnamon," came next. And finally, Key Lime, a mouth-watering "moist cake with a lime flavor, a citrus tart lime curd filling and lime cream cheese frosting," finished off the tasting. Even though the samples were small, following that sweet consumption Sofia was experiencing sugar overload. The *demitasse* of espresso was the perfect end to a perfect tasting day.

When they boarded the bus for the return trip to north Dallas, apprehension picked at Sofia. As she thought about returning home, she wondered, *What fresh hell awaits?*

~

After the fun, yet tiring day of touring chocolate shops, Sofia sat on her deck to unwind. She was relaxed. She put her feet up on one of the zero-gravity lawn chairs. The lacey shadows from her backyard trees undulated in the timid breeze, complementing the peaceful moment. Suddenly, the black plastic cover of one of Jet's windows was snatched back, and there was Jet, looking straight at her, as if he was checking on her. The man never ceases to amaze. Sofia's neck tightened as if it became a part of an armor worn to protect her from the violent sensations she felt when Jet was near. The black plastic fell back in place, and Sofia relaxed a bit until the next time he made his presence known.

~

While Sofia and Maria spent the day in chocolate consumption, Jet worked for hours on his next project. Since Taylor had her lunch delivered every day, and always with a tall glass of iced tea, he had a demonic plan that would add to her emotional distress.

He laid his supplies out on his kitchen table and gazed at them like a loving father: a bag of psilocybin – those so-called 'magic mushrooms' that make a person high but also induce paranoia in those prone to it when taken regularly. He had also laid out a rolling pin borrowed from Taylor. Destiny was not the type of woman to have a rolling pin or even know what it was. Her talents lay far from the kitchen. That's what Jet loved about her. He organized his supplies on the kitchen table: rolling pin, very small scissors, clear, two-sided tape in a handy dispenser, a tiny funnel, and dozens of little sugar packets like those used in restaurants to sweeten coffee or tea.

The mushrooms had been dried so they would break into small crumbs when Jet carefully smashed them with the rolling pin. He attached a jeweler's loupe (also borrowed) to his glasses to magnify his work. This had to be perfect. He had learned patience and the ability to work with small items, such as flower seeds, while in prison, so he felt this would be a piece of cake if he just stayed focused.

He used the tiny fingernail scissors to cut a precise opening at one end of a sugar packet, then shook the contents out and into a trash can. He took a small pile of mushrooms, smoothed them out into one layer, and ran the rolling pin over them. Magic, indeed! He was on a roll – pun intended. He stomped around in a circle gleefully.

When crushed, the mushrooms looked exactly like the raw, brown natural sugar that one finds in those small envelopes. He smiled and hummed as he inserted the tiny funnel into the now empty packet. With his other hand, he scooped up enough crushed mushrooms to fill the natural sugar packet. Then he stuck a piece of two-sided tape just inside the opening and squeezed it shut. *Voila! My God, I'm a genius. No one will take the time to see the opening has been tampered with.*

After a few hours, his neck and back were in pain, but he had enough packets for at least a week. He put his supplies away and could not wait for the delivery person to bring Taylor's lunch tomorrow.

Jet watched from his front window every day so he could catch the lunch delivery person. He used his best stealth-like ninja moves to head off the delivery. He put on a big smile and greeted the person.

Then he'd say, "I'm helping Miss. Taylor so I'll take her lunch to her."

They were always happy to hand it off. Taylor was not a favorite with delivery people, and it was a known fact that she did not tip.

When Jet had the lunch bag and large container of tea, he quickly rustled around in the bag to remove any sugar packets there and replace them with his works of art. In his opinion, this would add a fun element to the already crazy old lady. He quietly placed Taylor's lunch in front of her door and rang the doorbell. Then he slipped away.

The project was a success. Taylor became more agitated and made more frequent accusations of psychological warfare. The mushrooms were doing their work.

~

Sofia concentrated on writing an article about the chocolate shop bus tour. It flowed effortlessly and resulted in a tantalizing description of the chocolates they had sampled. It was informative and provided great publicity for the shops she wrote about. Glossy pictures accompanied the article. Some of the pictures were provided by the chocolate shops, and others were taken with Sofia's camera phone. She emphasized gift boxes wrapped and decorated especially for the upcoming Thanksgiving and Christmas holidays.

Her editor at *Chocotouring* magazine was enthralled with the unexpected story that highlighted local businesses and shop owners in various areas of Dallas. The tidbit about the building Bonnie and Clyde frequented was icing on the cake and sure to initiate some conversations. She promised Sofia she would send complimentary copies of the magazine to each of the chocolatiers.

Chapter 16 – The Nudist Neighbor and The Alley Crash

Sofia heard that Destiny had left Jet but didn't know whether to believe it or not. Then on a cool, crisp November day, Jet strolled across Sofia's yard and sat down on her deck with her. He told her Destiny had broken up with him and moved out while he was in jail. She was mad that he was incarcerated again, but she had been a guest at the county jail herself. Silly bitch didn't know how to hide her drugs. That didn't seem to count though, when they got into an argument. Everything was Jet's fault.

He had received a notice to vacate the duplex from the City of Dallas. Eloise had told him she was working on it, but he didn't believe it would really happen. She had been threatening eviction in two weeks for the last four months. This morning there it was, notice of eviction taped to his front door. He was supposed to be out within 48 hours. That would not be possible, but he'd start packing and planned to get out as soon as he could. Nigel and Frank were on their own. Their names were not on the eviction notice, so they had said they were not going anywhere. They had paid their rent to Jet and would stay right there until the end of the month.

Sofia was elated to hear that Jet would be moving in a few days. As for Nigel and Frank, she would leave that mess to Eloise, but they would have to move soon, too. Maybe the neighborhood would get back to normal with no ex-cons, exotic dancers, or FBI men. She laughed when she asked Annalise what they could talk about then.

~

The little alley that ran behind the houses on Shadow Lane and gave access to their garages had seen a lot of action, but nothing quite like this. In the middle of the night, a car jumped the curb, drove over a corner of Sofia's yard, and plowed through a brick retaining wall on the other side of the alley. It went over a large flower bed and crashed into the neighbor's garage door. Pieces of a lime green fender and silver bumper lay in the alley. It had to be a fierce impact. Incredibly, someone had been able to drive away supposedly unhurt, but that's what happened. It was even more remarkable that no one heard the crash. It was only discovered when dog owners were out for an early morning walk with their pets the next day.

By evening, everyone on Shadow Lane had heard about the crash in the alley. The damage was to the home of a single, older man who was rumored to be wealthy. His house was the largest in all of Shadow Canyon. His yard was impeccable, but he was somewhat of a recluse. Sofia had only seen him once, and that was enough. While walking Truffles and Bon Bon, she glanced over at his backyard, only to regret it seconds later. He was sitting by his pool completely nude. His eyes were shut so he probably assumed no one could see him. Just like her dogs think no one can see them when they hide their faces in their blankets. Sofia quickly turned away and saw one of his gardeners smiling at her.

His tanned face was pleasant and almost apologetic when, with a Mexican accent, he said, "Senora, he usually wears boxers when we are around."

Sofia smiled and tried not to blush as she said, "Thank you."

Crazy neighborhood!

Several people had come out to see the damage in the alley. Flashlight in hand, Sofia decided to join them. She walked slowly toward the group of shadowy figures standing at the end of the alley. She approached carefully, but as she got nearer to the group, she saw it was all neighbors. They were chatting about their guess as to what had happened. The owner of the damaged home was nowhere to be seen.

Annalise stood beside Sofia, and they joined the conversation about how no one heard it in the middle of the night. They all agreed the driver of the lime green vehicle was not someone who lived in the neighborhood because they didn't know of anyone having anything on four wheels in that color. Another mystery, but better left to the police to investigate.

Sofia said, "The police are here so often, they're going to start charging us."

Taylor was a few feet away but heard the comment. She scooted over close to them and asked, "Are you talking about me calling the police? Well, I don't believe Jet is really moving away, so I may very well have to call them again!"

Sofia and Annalise muttered, "Sure, Taylor, call anytime you need them."

Taylor thought for a moment and then added, "And I believe it was him who caused this damage. He was probably high on the drugs he uses. He must have been driving a friend's car."

Her accusations of Jet will never end.

By the next day, the mess was all cleaned up in the alley, the retaining wall was replaced, and the neighbor's garage was repaired. Sofia thought that was very cool but realized when you're rich, people rush to work for you.

Taylor repeatedly insisted it was Jet who crashed in the alley. He didn't have a lime green vehicle that we know of, but he could have borrowed someone else's. Before he moved from Duplex A, he saw Taylor in the back yard and told her some of the things she wonders about, she'll be able to figure out, but there are other things she will never understand. The accident in the alley might be one of them. She decided she would continue to sleep with all her outside lights on and her knife in her hand.

Sofia later heard from Annalise it was a guy who lived in a nearby apartment who had crashed. The police spotted his car in the parking lot and were able to find him. They contacted the nudist, and he agreed to not press charges if the guy would just pay for the repairs. Agreed. All was well in the neighborhood again.

With Destiny gone and Jet on the way out, Sofia felt the drama would subside. Jet was the only thing Taylor complained about, so she should be quiet now. But that was not to be. Taylor soon called Sofia late one night and said someone was in the alley opening and closing the bed of their truck. She thought it was Jet, and he was doing it to taunt her. Sofia asked her if she was going to look outside and see what it was. She said no, she would not give him that satisfaction. As far as he knows, she's not bothered at all. In reality, she stood in her bedroom, stiff with apprehension, knife in hand, but grateful that Sofia was home and was talking to her.

She hung up and climbed back into bed, eyes wide open. She soon heard footsteps in the attic and whispered to herself, "I knew he wasn't gone."

~

About this same time, the police assisted Frank and Nigel in vacating the duplex, and a new fence was miraculously built, providing Sofia with a little more privacy and peace of mind. She did a little happy dance at the prospect that her life would get better. She was able to let the dogs out by themselves since her backyard was now enclosed on all four sides. It was completely safe for Truffles and Bon Bon. She could enjoy sitting on her deck with a good book or just soaking up the sun again. She would feel comfortable in a bathing suit next spring.

She was looking forward to the holidays but sometimes wished she had a significant other to enjoy them with. Her friendly neighbor Greg had sold his house very quickly, and he had moved on. Whoever the new owners were, they kept to themselves and were never seen outdoors in their yard. Sofia and Greg had promised to keep in touch, but he had moved to Ft. Worth, so that wouldn't be easy. It's only 30 miles from Dallas, but with traffic, it can be an hour's drive. Sofia wasn't familiar with Ft. Worth and had no reason to go there. She knew she would probably never see Greg again, especially if he was successful in finding a new friend. She wasn't exactly sad, just a little bit lonely. The holidays always brought that out in her, and it was only a few days until the season began with Thanksgiving.

Chapter 17 – The FBI and Agent Lawson

The main FBI office for Dallas, Texas was in an area near downtown but not too easy to find. The big sign near the front door, *Department of Justice*, glistened in the sunlight. The building had the appearance of most Government buildings – no nonsense. There were no outdoor gardens or seating areas. Leisurely strolling or loitering was not encouraged.

    Preston Lawson had driven to Dallas from Houston with suitcases full of clothes in the trunk of his car, beside his attaché and the long gun that was secured in its case. He was strapped; that is, he wore his pistol in a shoulder holster under his suit coat, always within reach. He found the FBI office with the help of his GPS and parked in the Visitor's parking area as close to the front door as possible. He sat in his car, assessing the building and surrounding area. It was a habit, something a man in his position had to do to stay safe, sometimes to stay alive. His perfectly chiseled face was serious under dark aviator glasses. Hard to tell from his demeanor if he was a good guy or a bad guy.

    He entered the building and strode down the long hall, locked offices on either side, with a confident air that said *don't mess with me.*

He approached the receptionist at the end of the hall, a pretty girl whose toes curled at the sight of him. He introduced himself, and the receptionist said she would be happy to show him where he needed to go. She stepped in front of him and led him, hips swaying, to an office marked Special Agent in Charge.

She unlocked the door and gave the key to Preston. Her hot pink lips parted as she smiled, "See you later. Let me know if there's anything I can do for you."

The office was in synch with the rest of the building – no nonsense. It had a basic desk and chair and framed inspirational quotes on the beige walls. He was ok with all of it. He had grown up amidst opulence and didn't need it in an office.

His transfer from Houston was a well-deserved reward for his years of crime fighting. He had no trouble getting a job with the FBI right after college. He was good at it and had been working undercover for the last two years. His efforts resulted in the largest fentanyl bust ever in Houston. The fentanyl came in with mules and human traffickers from Mexico every week, and it was killing Americans, a lot of them just kids. Preston worked tirelessly to get it off the streets and school campuses in Houston, and now he would do the same in Dallas.

The big bust he orchestrated had given him rock star status at the FBI, and he was promoted to Special Agent in Charge of Dallas. It had helped ruin his marriage, but there were other factors, too. He would never resent the time he spent on the job.

After Preston got settled in his new office, a masculine-looking female agent came in and asked him if he was ready to meet his team. She took him (no hips swaying) to a large room with tables and desks crammed in every inch of it. It smelled like hard work. There were computers and monitors on each desk. Large maps and mug shots lined the walls. There was no symmetry to their arrangement; they were functional only.

About a dozen agents were there working their shifts on computers, speaking on phones, or in conversations with other agents. It was the noisy din of a very busy place. Black jackets with large yellow letters that spelled FBI hung from the backs of chairs and coat racks. There was a horseshoe-shaped table with one agent and a dozen monitors. The monitors displayed charts and graphs of various sizes and styles. Preston wasn't sure what function they served, but he would be sure to ask. The men and women were dressed in slacks and long-sleeved white shirts. Some of them were strapped with their shoulder holsters, ready for duty should they be needed.

Preston made a very short speech about being happy to join them and pledged to meet with each of them individually in the near future. He said he had already been briefed on the files that were being worked. He had decided to take the one of June Thibadeau himself since he had interviewed her in south Texas after her claim of being kidnapped by a drug-related gang.

June had worked on a secret FBI project, and her mental condition had been called into question. She retired and moved to Dallas and was under surveillance. The FBI wanted to be sure she had no ties to drug gangs or anyone else who might be interested in obtaining information about her work in the Gulf of Mexico. Preston said he would take surveillance of Ms. Thibadeau to familiarize himself with her current surroundings and activities.

But most of his work would be putting fentanyl drug dealers out of business. June had reported that the men who kidnapped her had fentanyl. He wanted to be sure they had not coerced her into their deadly business. A death threat would often turn innocent citizens into drug dealers or mules. After his short speech, he went back to his office, and the agents went back to work.

His office was quiet as he looked around it. He became conscious of the fact he was completely alone. On his own, he would have to work hard to achieve the success he had in Houston. His mind wandered to his parents and what they would think of his new position and surroundings. A warm smile crossed his face as he thought of how his mother would want to redecorate his office for sure. His father would probably appear stoic and offer only a "good job."

He leaned back in his chair and put his feet up on his desk. He wanted to take a moment to review his life and how he got to this place. His father was an oil company executive in Houston who brought home tons of money and the aroma of other women's perfumes. He never had much time for Preston or his mother.

But, she seemed happy with her constant shopping and trips to the beach to help save the turtles. It allowed her to get away from the pressure of Houston society. Even with her busy life, she always had time to give Preston the love he needed and the material things he wanted. Preston resented his father, which spurred him to work out every day and take every self-defense class he could find. He developed an impressive, muscled physique and vowed he would be a distinguished law enforcement officer someday. Righting wrongs was very important to him.

He had put in a long day with the five-hour drive from Houston and a few hours in his new office. He said goodnight to those still working at 6 p.m. He drove to the upscale hotel nearby, where he had a reservation. He was not familiar with the area, but the online description of the hotel and surrounding area had drawn him in. It boasted walking distance to upscale dining and retail options and proximity to the downtown arena, where major sports games were played.

He was sure the hotel would do nicely until his furniture and other personal belongings were shipped up to Dallas for an apartment he had yet to find. Elegant apartments and condos with views of downtown Dallas surrounded the hotel and might provide the perfect residence for him. He was looking for low maintenance and easy access to his office, but if it happened to be luxurious, so much the better.

~

Preston spent a few boring days in surveillance of Shadow Lane and June Thibadeau, aka Taylor. He listened to the tapes that had been recorded from the listening devices planted in her duplex. He was concerned with her visit to the gun show and subsequent conversations that indicated she would buy a handgun. There had been enough shootings in the Dallas area for him to take her comments seriously. He wanted to determine if she was a threat or, as she said, getting a handgun purely for protection.

One of the neighbors had noticed him parked in front of her house and had questioned him. Without hesitation, he showed her his badge. He hoped she would not tell Jet or Taylor that he was there. But he didn't ask her to keep quiet because, in his experience, that was the best way to get someone to tell all their friends.

He had studied the condition of high-pressure neurological syndrome. There was a case of it recently that the Houston FBI office identified. They had gotten help for the man suffering from it by sending him to a government-run psych facility. He had developed high-pressure neurological syndrome after spending time in a submersible, a small submarine. Taylor had spent three days on and four days off from her FBI job that required her to work while in a submersible in the Gulf of Mexico. The cover story was that the crew was studying marine life, but Preston knew it was a cover for something Top Secret, Classified. He was a tough guy, but he couldn't imagine how anyone could exist in a small submersible. It seemed to him that anyone subjected to those conditions would develop psychological issues sooner or later, and he had great sympathy for those who did.

Chapter 18 – The Taylor Meltdown and Ghost in the Attic

Sofia had been naïve to think life near Taylor would be quiet after Jet and Destiny moved. It was only a few days later when Sofia heard a blood-curdling scream coming from Taylor's direction. She had run to the middle of the street, fallen to her knees, and was sobbing uncontrollably with her face in her hands. Her whole body was shaking, and her chest was heaving. Sofia jumped into a pair of shoes and ran out her front door. Annalise and two other neighbors were already in the street, trying to console Taylor.

Words began to tumble out, but no understandable sentences. Annalise's husband had joined the group. He reached down and gently brought Taylor to her feet. Annalise and Sofia put their arms around her and gave her a few minutes to calm down. She finally removed her hands from her face to reveal the look of sheer terror that remained.

Sofia's heart broke for her. What could have caused this? Sofia asked if Taylor would like to come to her house and sit down. She agreed, so Sofia and Annalise held her close, one on each side of her, guiding her by her elbows into Sofia's living room. Truffles and Bon Bon were quite curious when they walked in, but Sofia put them in their crates, and they stared out from there.

Sofia gave Taylor a glass of cold water and asked if she would like anything stronger. Taylor said no, but Annalise said she and Sofia would need something after this was over. Taylor's body stopped shaking as she sipped on the glass of water. Then the words turned to sentences, and the story came out between gasps for breath.

Taylor had heard a noise in her attic and decided to be brave enough to take a look. She stood on a small stepladder and unlocked the padlock on the attic door. She pulled the attic ladder down and started to climb up when she saw a man poke his face into the opening. That's when she screamed. She fell backwards off the ladder and had a painful landing, crashing against a wall in the hallway.

The new 22-caliber pistol she held in her hand fired three shots. No one knew she had bought the gun, and this was the first time it had been fired. Taylor jerked with each loud shot that hit the ceiling near the attic opening. White dusty debris fell from the ceiling and covered her, making her look like a deranged snowman. She struggled to her feet and left the gun behind as she ran out of her house, only stopping when she reached the middle of the street. At that point, she was so terrified she couldn't move.

Annalise asked, "Who was it? Who was the man up in your attic? Was it Jet?"

"No, not Jet."

"Who fired gunshots, Taylor?"

"It was me. It was a misfire. I'm not used to my new gun yet."

Annalise was obviously upset and began to pace the floor. She said, "That S.O.B. Jet! He probably rented the attic to someone who's been living up there! If he hasn't run away, we'll have the police go up and take care of him!"

Taylor mumbled it would not be necessary to call the police this time.

Annalise and Sofia were confused. "Why not?"

"It's just not! OK?"

Annalise and Sofia didn't know what to do. They wrung their hands and jumped nervously when, within minutes two Dallas police officers were knocking on Sofia's door. Annalise's husband had called them. They asked if Taylor was there and if they could speak to her. Taylor did not look happy, but Sofia said, of course, they could come in. They politely approached Taylor and got her permission to ask a few questions. They asked if she could describe the man she saw in her attic.

"No, not very well. I was so scared."

"Can you tell us his hair color, his skin color, anything distinctive about him?"

Taylor began to sob and shake again. After some gentle encouragement from the officers, Taylor composed herself and spoke so softly that no one in the room was sure they had heard her.

"I might as well tell the truth. It was my husband," Taylor whispered.

Annalise fell backward into a chair. Sofia looked on in a confused state. The police asked Taylor why her husband would scare her so badly.

"He's ..... dead."

"When did he die? Is his body in your attic?"

"He died three years ago in Monroe."

"Could it be someone else who looks like him?"

Taylor became impatient. "No! I know what my husband looks like, and it was him that I saw! Oh, how could this be happening? An old voodoo priestess told me he would haunt me. I don't know if y'all believe in that stuff, but I do. I've seen things in Louisiana that no human can explain.

"Do you think he's going to haunt me forever? I'm so sorry I MADE him work in the attic that day. It was too hot, and I knew he had not been feeling well. I'll never forgive myself! And maybe he won't either."

The police officers gave a knowing look to each other before one of them kindly asked Taylor if she thought she had seen an apparition. She started sobbing again, and Sofia asked if there was anything she could do or anyone she should call.

"No, there's no one."

It had been nearly an hour since she screamed and ran out of her house, and only now could she tell them clearly what had happened to her husband.

After straightening her body in the chair, Taylor explained, "It's my own fault. When we had a house in Monroe, Louisiana, I made my husband help me clean out the attic there on a very hot summer day.

"He complained about tightness in his chest, but he looked fine to me. He was sort of a hypochondriac, so I didn't pay much attention. After a couple of hours, he sat down on a cardboard box, took several deep gasps for air, and then fell on the floor. All I could think about was the dust he had stirred up. I asked what was wrong, and he couldn't answer. He was rolling back and forth and writhing in pain.

"I went down the attic ladder to the phone in the bedroom and dialed 911. Two EMTs arrived just a few minutes later and went up into the attic to look after him."

The EMTs had worn name badges; one said *Billy Ricky,* and the other said *Samue*l. They were very agile, and apparently, they were among Monroe's finest in crisp uniforms laden with badges and pins.

They nodded and spoke respectfully to Taylor. She had climbed the ladder to direct them to her husband's body among the many packed boxes stacked two or three deep. One small shaft of light showed through the boards in the attic floor but did not provide any light on the body, now stiffened. Overall, the attic was dusty and dark with a musty smell.

The EMTs opened and closed their eyes to adjust to their surroundings and then turned on their flashlights. They spoke into their recorder that he was dead after they examined the body, checked for a pulse, and knelt close to his face to check his breathing.

Taylor sobbed as they discussed how to best get him down from the attic and into the ambulance. Samuel went back down the ladder and scooted a stretcher close to the bottom of it. Billy Ricky would slide the body down feet first, and Samuel would catch him and get him on the stretcher. Most unfortunately, Billy Ricky lost his grip as the body dangled over the attic opening. The deceased husband rattled and banged down the ladder and landed face-up in a twisted mess on top of Samuel.

Samuel yelled, "Fer Chrissake, Billy Ricky! Git him offa me!"

Taylor screamed and turned away, but before she did, she got a glimpse of her husband's body with glassy eyes staring at her. The sight that still haunts her today. The EMTs managed to get him out of the house and took him to the hospital, where he was officially declared DOA, Dead on Arrival.

Taylor looked pleadingly at Sofia and Annalise, "I swore I'd never have another attic, but the duplex was so cute, I couldn't resist. I guess this explains all the noises I've heard in the attic, but now what do I do?"

Everyone in the room remained deathly still, looking at Taylor, and in some state of shock at the story she had told and her appearance with white snowflake-like ceiling material covering her. Sofia and Annalise were speechless. That didn't happen very often, but they were both shaken by the stunning revelations from Taylor. They had never heard anything about her husband or the idea he was haunting her.

They were not sure if this let Jet off the hook for all the other things Taylor had complained about or not. Maybe Taylor's husband's ghost was responsible for all the things Sofia had dismissed as figments of Taylor's imagination; the noises, the dirty socks, antifreeze, and everything else.

Sofia was not one to discount the possibility of paranormal activity but had never experienced it herself. She was tired of the mysteries and was ready for some solid answers. Maybe they would be forthcoming now that Taylor had opened up to the police. The events of today would take some time to process. She wondered if Taylor's recounting of her husband's death would ever be validated as true and accurate.

The police officers said they would walk Taylor home and search the attic for any signs of someone being there today or in the recent past. They said phroggers will always leave a blanket, water, food, or something that gives a clue as to who was there and when.

Taylor asked, "What's a phrogger?"

"That's the name given to people who secretly stay in attics or even in closets in a house while the owner still lives there."

"Oh, my goodness," said Taylor, "you mean that really happens."

Both police officers responded at the same time, "More often than you might think."

Taylor said she needed to lie down and would prefer to stay with Sofia for a while rather than be home alone after the police completed their search. Sofia got her some blankets and pillows and told her she was welcome to spend the night, no matter what the police found. It was not what Sofia had hoped for, but Taylor said she would love to stay.

The police officers walked over to Taylor's duplex and made a thorough search. There was nothing suspicious or out of place in the living areas downstairs. They went into the attached garage and looked around but found only tools, paint, and Taylor's laundry. When they reached the back hallway, the entry to the attic was still open. They went up the ladder single file with flashlights in hand. After crawling through the opening, they stood back-to-back and moved their flashlights to see every inch of the attic.

There were dust bunnies on the floor and a couple of cobwebs in the corners, but nothing to suggest a human or non-human had been there. They removed the cover to a ceiling vent and called out into the blackness of the air duct. There was no answer, but it was much too small for any person to wiggle through anyway. If it did connect with the outside, it would not allow access to the attic from the roof. Nothing, absolutely nothing, stirred in the attic. No evidence such as food, drinks, and blankets were left behind, as phroggers often do.

The officers went back to Sofia's house and told Taylor there was no reason to be fearful in her home. They did a complete search and felt sure it was secure.

"Be careful with that gun, m'am. No real damage this time, but you could have hurt yourself."

Taylor almost seemed disappointed, but she thanked them and said she'd still feel more comfortable sleeping on Sofia's couch that night.

They were all unaware that Preston Lawson, an FBI man, had witnessed Taylor's meltdown through the binoculars he kept in his car during stakeouts. He had seen some weird stuff in his career, and this ranked near the top of that list. He stayed in his unnoticed black FBI car and let the local police do their work. He would make a full report to Washington, but he thought it was time to bring Ms. Thibadeau in for some questioning.

He was relieved that the gunfire he heard had only damaged the ceiling, not a human. He knew she had a lethal kitchen knife under her pillow and kept the gun in her nightstand. Even though Taylor on many nights lay awake, waiting for Jet to give her a reason to use them. Preston saw no evidence that he ever would.

Chapter 19 – The Taylor Interview and Treatment

Preston arrived unannounced at Taylor's door. He flashed his FBI badge and asked if he could come in to talk. Taylor did not usually welcome uninvited guests, but Preston exuded masculinity in a polished professional package. She remembered him questioning her on the Gulf Coast, so she knew he was legit. She had not had a male companion for a long time, and if it was ever discussed, she would explain she was too old for that nonsense. However, upon seeing Preston, she thought, *Yeah, I'm old, but I'm not dead!*

She invited him to come in and tugged at her shirt, wishing she was wearing something nicer. Her hair was in tight curls that she had not brushed out yet today.

Preston graciously thanked her, adding, "Nice to see you again, Miss Thibadeau."

Her eyelashes fluttered as she motioned to a chair. "Please sit down. Would you like tea?"

Preston declined the tea and instead dove into his reason for being there. He asked what she had been doing in Dallas. Her answer was evasive as expected. In their further conversation, it became clear that Taylor thought Preston had been watching Jet and was there to discuss the many grievances she had about him.

Instead, he eased the conversation around to her previous work for the FBI and her kidnapping near the Gulf of Mexico. She did not offer any new information. When he asked her if she had any contact with the kidnapping gang members and if she had ever tried fentanyl, anger jumped out from her face.

He calmly told her fentanyl has become such a problem in Texas he must follow up on any lead. She leaped out of her chair and marched back and forth across the room. The room was filled with dainty furniture, frilly lampshades, and old-fashioned doilies. Her behavior at that moment was in stark contrast to her gentile surroundings.

"Sorry to upset you, Ms. Thibadeau. Please understand I'm just doing my job."

"Oh, yeah," she nodded her head aggressively. "I understand, alright! You don't think much of me. You forget all that I did for the FBI."

"No, ma'am, we will never forget the good work you did. I just have a couple more questions for you. Could you please sit down so we can finish this up?"

Reluctantly, Taylor sat down and faced Preston again. When he asked if she had ever heard of high-pressure neurological syndrome and how it causes paranoia in some, she clenched her lips and nearly choked on her words.

"It's time for you to go, Mr. Lawson."

It had hit her like a ton of bricks - the FBI was watching *her*, not Jet! Preston was not there out of concern for her. He didn't care that Jet had been tormenting her. He suspected her of something illegal! She broke out in little beads of sweat and paced the room again, worried about what might be next.

Preston left, but while still in his car, he contacted the Houston office to see if there was any new gang activity that would validate Taylor's kidnapping story. He wanted to give her every benefit of the doubt. There was nothing new to substantiate her claim.

Back in his office, he prepared the paperwork to bring Taylor in for psychological testing. After a restless night, he returned to her house the next day, paperwork in hand, and explained it was sort of a formality. He was obligated to test anyone who had shown signs of emotional stress. She reminded him she no longer works for the FBI, but he said they had the authority to test employees and private citizens alike. After she slammed her knitting down in anger, she stomped her feet on the floor like a child would do. He put his hand on her shoulder and reassured her everything was alright. Then he escorted her to his car and drove her to the FBI facility.

While she was away, Drug Enforcement Agency officers executed their search warrant and tossed her residence for fentanyl. It's rare that a drug gang would let a person escape them and then never hunt them down later, probably to recruit them for drug sales. That is, if they decided that was more valuable than killing that person. It was necessary to find out all they could about Taylor for FBI reasons and also for her protection.

The DEA officers were unable to find anything in her home. Meanwhile, she passed the drug test at the FBI lab. Preston was somewhat surprised. But he approved the request to send her to a government-run facility for help with paranoia. He thought about it for a couple of hours before he approved it. He knew the paranoia could have been caused by her time in the submersible doing her job. He felt sympathy for her but, in the end, knew he was doing the right thing.

Jet heard all about the search of Taylor's duplex and her admittance for psychological testing from his sister, Lolita. Again, news traveled the entire Shadow Lane neighborhood. He laughed when he heard she passed the FBI drug test. He knew no one would detect the psilocybin, the magical mushrooms he loved and had secretly shared with Taylor.

That was one of the great things about psilocybin: they're not detected in a routine drug test. He had learned this from a fellow inmate while in prison. It was a tidbit of information he had tucked away for future use. A test must be designed specifically to look for them, and the FBI had no reason to think of that for Taylor.

He had told Taylor there were some things he did that she would never figure out. This was one of them.

Chapter 20 – The Dinner with Lawson

Sofia was deep in thought, taking a break from the book she had been reading, when she heard her front doorbell ring. She was surprised to see a drop-dead gorgeous man standing at her door when she opened it. She would open her door for this guy any day. She felt the same sensation she had when she first saw the stuntman, but this man had the aura of a rich guy. She couldn't imagine who he was or why he was there.

"Miss Sofia Lanera?"

"Yes."

"I'm sorry to bother you, but I'm Special Agent Lawson with the FBI."

Sofia thought, *you sure are,* before she answered, "No problem. You're not bothering me."

"I wonder if I could come in and talk to you about your neighbors in Duplex A and B."

"Of course, there's probably a lot to talk about."

Agent Lawson told her first of all she should not be worried about Jet. They, the FBI, were aware of his existence, but he was a small-time criminal in their eyes. They would leave it to the local police to deal with him if he violated parole again, which he probably would. He had spent his life so far getting into trouble and serving time. But Lawson didn't think he was any threat to Sofia, and he was now staying with a friend in a town several miles away. So, he would probably find other people, places, and things to darken.

No, Agent Lawson wanted to tell Sofia what they knew about June Thibadeau, the woman in Duplex B. But Sofia could hardly concentrate on anything he said. His brilliant gray eyes, the color of tornado skies, were mesmerizing. When he asked her what she knew about June, she was able to focus and tell him she went by the name of Taylor here, her maiden name. She either retired or quit a government job down on the Gulf. After retirement, she bought Duplex B and had been harassed by Jet from the day she moved in. She had told Sofia recently about the harrowing ordeal of being kidnapped before she left her job and moved to Dallas.

There was little emotion on the agent's face when he told her part of what she knew was true, but part of it was not. He had been on a stakeout to watch Taylor, not Jet, these past few days. She had worked on a sensitive FBI project and had spent time in a submersible, a tiny submarine, as part of her research in the Gulf of Mexico. She began acting strangely a few months ago, and her superiors had sent her for medical testing.

It turned out she was suffering from high-pressure neurological syndrome, which causes paranoia. It happens occasionally to people who do not adjust well to being in a submarine. The FBI gave her some time off to rest and decompress. When she went back to work, she told the story of being kidnapped as she was leaving the facility on land near the beach.

They sent her back for more medical and psych evaluation. It was determined she had a very severe case of paranoia and was not responding well to the medication she was given. Since her work was of a sensitive nature, possibly relating to our national security, it was time for her to leave the government service.

Retirement with full benefits was offered to her, and she accepted. Under the circumstances, the FBI wanted to know she was not now being contacted by or meeting with any foreign government representatives or the gang that kidnapped her – if that story was true. The FBI had never been able to verify it.

Since Preston had interviewed her in Houston, it was decided he would pick up the case when he transferred to Dallas. And that's how he happened to be in the right place at the right time to witness her meltdown and startling claim that her ex-husband's ghost was in her attic. He had sat in his car with binoculars focused on Taylor as she ran into the street and collapsed into a blubbering mess.

Sofia could hardly believe what she was hearing. She was still processing the information when Agent Lawson continued. "We have taken Ms. Thibadeau to a treatment facility where she will get the help she needs in a caring and professional environment.

"Since you are now her nearest neighbor, we wanted you to know that she is being taken care of, and you will not see or hear from her for a while. You are safe not only from Jet but also from the rants of Miss Thibadeau. We had a listening device on her phone and a couple of others in her house. We know she has made an alarming number of accusations about Jet. While he's no choir boy, he has not done anything offensive to Miss Thibadeau.

"*Everything* she told you about him is untrue. Her thoughts about Jet are the result of her paranoia. She literally scared herself silly. As far as we can tell, he never entered her house and certainly did not spend his nights in her attic."

Sofia's shoulders drooped as she let out a loud sigh. This information about Taylor was incredible, but there were times she had doubts about Taylor herself. She felt stupid for believing and sympathizing with her, especially about the kidnapping. That had haunted her for days. She had even told Taylor she could stay with her if she was afraid at any time.

Sofia was visibly shaken by the information Preston gave her. Her hands and her voice trembled. "I was so worried for her. I offered to let her stay in my house. I would have taken care of her, comforted her, fed her, and hopefully restored her strength and sense of security. I guess I was being foolish."

Agent Lawson's voice lowered, "No, not at all. You seem like a kind and caring person. Is there anything I can do or tell you to make you feel better?"

She shook her head no. "I just need some time to think about all this."

"I won't be in your neighborhood any longer. With Jet and Miss Thibadeau both removed from the duplex next to you, there is no need for FBI surveillance."

Sofia's blue eyes welled up with tears. She wasn't sure why, but it was probably a reflex of her feeling of relief. The agent assured her the threats and mystery she had experienced were over. She could feel safe in her home and safe to leave it when she wanted to. She thanked him for filling her in with the statuses of Jet and Taylor – still Taylor to her. She smiled and said it might take a while for her to get used to the calm that would result from her neighbors' absences.

"I understand." Preston continued, "If you don't think I'm being unprofessional, I'd like to take you to dinner tomorrow evening to help you relax your nerves and move on. I can answer any questions you think of between now and then."

Whoa, there was a flutter in Sofia's stomach as she imagined sitting across from Mr. FBI in a romantic restaurant with deep rich wine and candles. Her imagination was very much intact, regardless of how stressed or scared she was.

"I'd like that, whether it's unprofessional or not. It seems your case here is over, so I don't see any reason we can't have dinner. And I very well might have more questions by then. I need a little time to think right now."

"I'm glad you feel that way. I'll pick you up around 7:00 tomorrow evening if that works for you. Looking forward."

Agent Lawson shook her hand in a professional way and walked out her front door. Perhaps the handshake was to make her feel better about having dinner with him tomorrow night. But she didn't care if it was unprofessional or not. He had awakened an interest she thought might be dead after her experience with the stuntman in L.A.

Life had turned a corner for Sofia. Duplex A was listed for sale, and extensive remodeling was underway. Repairing the bullet holes in the hall ceiling was top priority. Jet, Destiny, and Taylor were gone. It was shaping up to be a delightful holiday season, and if the FBI man was a part of it, so much the better. A smile of contentment rested on her face.

~

Dinner was all she had hoped for and maybe a little more. The FBI man picked her up in his shiny luxury sedan, not the black car with darkly tinted windows he used on the stakeout. He had just come from work and wore a dark gray, perfectly fitted suit with a crisp white shirt, and fifty shades of blue tie. They made small talk on the way to the restaurant. He revealed he was the top agent for the Dallas area, recently divorced and recently transferred to Dallas from Houston. He asked her to call him Preston or Law, as most of his friends do, and said how happy he was to have this time with her.

They reached the festive, yet elegant Mexican restaurant and valet parked. Preston held the heavy wood door open for Sofia and then checked in with the maître 'd. There was a reserved table waiting for them. It was a booth with expensive-looking leather banquettes. Preston stood while Sofia slid across the leather seat. She thought she saw admiration in his eyes as she wiggled to keep her skirt down below her knees.

Dozens of lighted candles surrounded the dining room. Large, brightly colored Mexican pots held flowers and plants. Soft music with a Latino beat played in the background. Sofia looked around to take it all in and told Preston how much she loved it. They both ordered margaritas and sipped them while they perused the menu. Sofia was careful not to consider anything that would be messy and might drip on the dreamy see-through blouse she was wearing. She wore her best flesh-colored bra under it and was pretty sure Preston had noticed.

Well into her second margarita, she had Preston's full attention. He was a terrific date in that he seemed oblivious to everything but Sofia. He barely looked at the waitress when he asked her to keep the cold drinks coming. Sofia felt confident enough to ask if he could tell her any more about Taylor and what kind of work she was doing.

He paused briefly, then, "I can tell you only because it's now public knowledge. It's on the Internet if you know where to search. The work was for the CIA. They developed a UUV, Unmanned Underwater Vehicle, that looked like a large catfish as part of a feasibility study. It was designed to collect water samples. The idea was that they could send it up a body of water to collect a water sample and return it to the CIA. The sample could be tested to see if it contained nuclear runoff or biochemical agents. With that information, they could tell what was going on in that specific location. Since it looked like a catfish, it would not arouse any suspicion.

"I'm not sure why, but it was never used. June conducted some renewed testing with it. Again, it has been decided not to use it. Too many other things of higher importance to work on. But DO NOT repeat this information to anyone. It's not classified, but no one really needs to know about it at this point."

Sofia appeared to be frozen in time. She held her margarita glass in one hand and stared at Preston across the table. Finally, she uttered, "Unbelievable. My neighbor Taylor was working on spy equipment! I would never have guessed."

"Exactly what we all wanted," Preston said gently. "Her appearance and persona were not what anyone would expect in an intelligence operation. Now please forget it, and let's get back to you and me."

Sofia tried to get the image of Taylor as a spy out of her head. She could only sip margaritas to accomplish that. It was a long and leisurely dinner that ended with them sharing a piece of avocado-chocolate cake. Sofia's head was spinning from the drinks and from the information about Taylor. Either way, she felt high as she bit into the avocado-chocolate cake. It was totally decadent, and she couldn't wait to tell Susan at *Chocotouring* magazine about it. She was going to pitch a story idea about unusual chocolate cakes.

Preston took her straight home after dinner. He was the perfect gentleman as he gave her a kiss on the cheek with no groping, although she wouldn't have minded. He told her he would call her and hoped to see her again soon. Then the big, shiny sedan drove off with Preston at the wheel, ready to solve other crimes. Sofia, a little tipsy, thought she might see a Batman symbol flash across the sky.

Chapter 21 – The Third Date

Preston had confided in Sofia that Taylor was going to sell her duplex. When she was released from treatment for high-pressure neurological syndrome, she did not want to return to the duplex. It was now a source of unpleasant memories. And she felt a little embarrassed that the whole neighborhood now knew of her emotional struggle. Sofia could certainly understand Taylor's feelings and was relieved to know she would not be returning to Shadow Lane.

With Jet and Destiny gone and the promise that Taylor would not return, Sofia anticipated a joyful, peaceful holiday season. She looked forward to Christmas and New Year's. She searched online for what to do on New Year's Eve in case Preston asked her to spend it with him. This year could end on a very positive note. She would not have expected the current set of circumstances a few weeks ago.

~

A few days later, Sofia smiled as she twirled around in front of her mirror. Her silk dress swished as she turned, and her earrings dangled jubilantly. She had a hot date with Preston Lawson, their third date, and we all know what that means. They were going for an early dinner and then to a concert at the enormous stadium that was the home of the Dallas football team. She sat down at her dressing table for a final check of her makeup. The tiny Yorkies approached her and looked up quizzically while she was humming. The doorbell rang, and that meant Preston was there. She popped up from her seat, switched off her bedroom light, and practiced her seductive stroll to the front door.

She greeted Preston, and he gave her a soft kiss on her cheek. They were running a bit late, so Sofia petted the dogs and said goodbye to them. She knew they would be fine if left out of their crates. The lights in the living room stayed on, but the rest of the house was dark. Preston opened the car door for Sofia, and they were soon just a set of tail lights on Shadow Lane. Truffles and Bon Bon retreated to their crates and pawed at their blankets to get them just right for the night's sleep.

A few seconds later, they both sat up and tilted their heads in the direction of Sofia's office. The curious little animals set off down the long, dark hall to find the source of the sounds they heard. The soft clicking of a computer keyboard became a little louder as they approached the office. They peered in and saw a man at Sofia's computer.

The man concentrated on his work, unaware the tiny puppies were watching him. His dark hair was as unkempt as the clothes he wore. The blue light from the computer screen was reflected in his dark-rimmed glasses. A grisly car wreck scene was displayed on the screen, and a vile sneer was on the man's face.

The dogs knew this man, so there was no barking. They turned away from him and returned to their crates with their little nails softly echoing off the hardwood floor.

One chapter of mysteries on Shadow Lane had closed, but another was about to open with terrifying implications for Sofia.

Made in the USA
Coppell, TX
09 August 2024